STONE'S

GINGER WINE

DOMINE DIRIGE NOS

STONE'S
GINGER WINE

Fortunes of a Family Firm

1740~1990

DAVID WAINWRIGHT

Quiller Press
London

Two future Chairmen of Finsbury Distillery: George Maxwell
(Grenadier Guards) and Peggy Bishop (ATS) in Oxford in 1939.

First published 1990 by
Quiller Press
46 Lillie Road
London SW6 1TN

ISBN 1 870948 34 3

Designed by Dale Dawson

Design and production in association with
Book Production Consultants, 47 Norfolk Street, Cambridge

Typeset by Cambridge Photosetting Services

Printed by The Bath Press, Avon

Contents

Foreword

*A*s we celebrate the 250th anniversary of the Finsbury Distillery, I find myself trying to compare our world of 1990 with that of 1740. The things we take for granted, or regard as essential, like the electric light, internal plumbing in houses, the speed and relative ease of communication and travel – all these, and many more, were still in the future. Indeed 1740 saw George Anson set off on his circumnavigation of the world, an adventure which was to last four years; James Cook, meanwhile, was twenty-five years away from the first of his great voyages. In France, the Montgolfier family were just celebrating the birth of their first son, who would become famous in years to come, along with his younger brother, for his pioneering flights in hot air balloons. On the other side of the Atlantic, George Washington was a mere boy. To the east, Russia, China and Japan had yet to become great actors on the world stage.

So it was that during George II's reign, and in the closing years of Sir Robert Walpole's time as Prime Minister (an office of which he was the first incumbent, and still retains the record for length of service, at twenty-one years), the business now known as Finsbury Distillery was established. Numerous businesses were most certainly started at around the same time and, as with any progeny, some were more healthy and striving than others. Finsbury was one of the strong ones which has survived through to the present day. What gives this story a special flavour is that one single family (the Bishop family) has steered and stayed with the business, and at the same time the business has stayed true to its last. The firm started as a producer and seller of alcoholic drinks and today that is what it continues to do.

It is often said by members of families who have inherited magnificent houses that they are custodians rather than owners and that their duty is to pass them on to their heirs in good order. The same could well have been said of my ancestors, except that the good and successful custodians have realized that, in business, it is not sufficient to sit and preserve your heritage; rather you must strive to move forward and grasp commercial reality, be it pleasant or not. Today, as part of a public limited liability company, it is of course a duty of the directors to act as custodians of the company's assets, but the unwritten imperative remains – to be commercial and to move forward. I would hope that on this basis someone, maybe a relative, will be able to write the foreword to the 300-year story of Finsbury as a thriving firm.

I began by making the point that the past 250 years have seen many significant achievements in human terms, and I would finish by observing that it is thanks to all the people who have worked for and given their best to Finsbury that our story is possible. It is, therefore, to those people that this book is dedicated.

Mrs G. C. Maxwell (née Bishop)
Chairman
1990

Introduction

*T*his book is about the Bishop family of London. It is also about the products with which they have been associated for at least 250 years. Many of those products are truly traditional, because they have been made consistently to recipes handed down from one generation to the next. The best known, and the one that continues to enjoy immense popularity and success today, is green ginger wine.

It was once, and indeed until a mere twenty years ago, part of a list that included all those country wines that are now only made, as they have been over the centuries, by individuals for their own and their families' and friends' consumption – elderflower, cowslip and the rest.

The curious fact is that the name of Bishop has not appeared on the label of the Finsbury Distillery's best-known product for well over a hundred years. The product is familiar and recognised as Stone's Original Green Ginger Wine. Joseph Stone was a retailer (in his time the leading retailer of Original Green Ginger Wine in London and the south of England), and thus the fact that this famous drink has carried his name since the mid-nineteenth century is one of the earliest examples of 'own brand' marketing.

The basic recipe for Original Green Ginger Wine remains as it has been for centuries. The only change is that while in past centuries the manufacturing process relied on the skilled judgement of individual foremen, developments in food chemistry and technology have enabled the process to be precisely gauged and scientifically controlled. The judgement of the makers is assisted by computers and electronic measuring instruments. It was once believed that the massive oak vats, one of them holding over 50,000 gallons and perhaps the largest in the world, imparted a particular flavour. Today the product can be matured in stainless steel. But while reliance is no longer only placed on the eye and taste of the individual in the making process, science and technology ensure a more consistent result.

The Bishop family have upheld this standard for 250 years, as distillers and vintners in the City of London. For most of that long period they were indeed distillers: they distilled London gin until 1971. They were also vintners, manufacturing British wines and importing foreign wines. The largest and most successful trade in British wines has been in what are known as 'sweets', defined in an Act of Parliament of William III in 1696 as

> liquors made by infusion, fermentation, or otherwise, from *foreign* fruit or sugar, or from fruit or sugar mixed with other materials, and commonly made use of for the recovering, increasing, or making of any kinds of wine or cider or any liquor called wine.

Meanwhile the wine that has been manufactured in Britain for many centuries is now known technically as 'made wine', since it is manufactured from imported dried fruit – raisins, currants or sultanas – macerated in water and then fermented. This is a process that dates back to the time of Charles I, when in 1635 one Francis Chamberleyne petitioned the King

> by his travell into forraigne parts, hath observed the making of wynes and dryed grapes, or raisons which wynes have been approved of by all such as have tasted the same . . . ; and ye pet [petitioner] having to his great

charges atteyned to the knowledge of the making thereof. His most humble suite to y^r Matie is; That you will be graciously pleased to grant unto him . . . under y^r Maties great seale of England for the sole making of the said wynes. . . .

The gentleman was granted his charter, while more recently 'made wine' has also been manufactured from imported grape juice or must, though not at Finsbury.

This book describes the history of the Bishop family in this trade, and the maintenance of traditional standards in a British drink that has been popular for at least 250 years.

STONE'S
SUPERIOR
TENT

STONE'S
SUPERIOR
RICH RAISIN

STONE'S
GINGER
TONIC WINE
JOSEPH STONE ON THE CORK LABEL WILL ALONE
GUARANTEE THE QUALITY.

STONE'S
SUPERIOR
GOOSEBERRY.

STONE'S
SUPERIOR
RASPBERRY

CHAPTER 1

The Long Tradition

T he name of Bishop has long been familiar in the craft of distilling, and in the City of London. Within the Bishop family it has been handed down from past generations that the company known as the Finsbury Distillery was founded in 1740. That date evidently had considerable legal importance to one branch of the Bishops as 'founding date'. But the family had the right to claim a much earlier start in the business. It has been proved that Bishops were distilling in the City of London long before 1740. The records of the Distillers' Livery Company show that in 1681 one George Bishop was apprenticed to Samuel Baker, a distiller of the City of London.

That was only forty years after the foundation of the Distillers' Livery Company in the last decade of the reign of Charles I, in order to raise the standards of a trade in which (in the words of the Guild's Letters Patent)

interlopers, who by their preposterous ways of working, and frequent use of base and unsound materials have brought scandal not only upon the works of this Art (the wares) but also upon the Art and Artists themselves. For suppression and future prevention of such delinquents, and their erroneous ways, and Relief and Reformation of the present Distillers, and their lawful successors, His Majesty hath been graciously pleased to supply us with the means to perform both.[1]

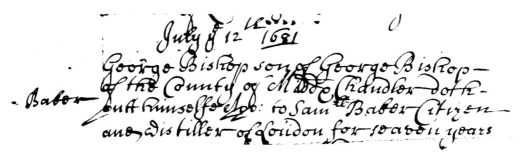

Extract from the records of the Distillers' Livery Company, showing the apprenticeship of George Bishop in 1681.

A decade later, the execution of the king and the assumption of power by Oliver Cromwell introduced ten years of puritanism that effectively damped down popular consumption of drink, along with other pleasures.

With the restoration of the monarchy in 1660, enjoyment became fashionable again, and the distillers set out to make their contribution. The origins of the craft are uncertain, but the distillation of spirits is thought to have been discovered in about the seventh century AD. The writings of Friar Bacon show that he knew about it in the thirteenth century; an author wrote a book on the preparation of alcohol and 'spirits of wine' in the same century. The perfect chemical separation of alcohol was apparently achieved in 1300 by a Montpellier physician, Arnauld de Villeneuve. In 1430 arrack was first imported into England from Genoa, and the import and home manufacture of spirituous liquors increased from that date.[2]

So young George Bishop in 1681 was learning a skill that was already well established in London. When he finished his apprenticeship, he started his own business in White's Alley in the Parish of St Giles, Cripplegate. So it may be that 1990 is not the 250th anniversary of the family business, but the 300th. By 1723 George's son Samuel had succeeded him, and their business was in Three Leg Court, Whitecross Street, where it remained until Samuel retired thirty years later.

The early years of the eighteenth century were flourishing times for the distillers, and for their colleagues and rivals the vintners. In particular, between 1734 and 1742 the manufacture of spirits on which excise duty was paid increased from 4,947,000 gallons to 7,160,000 gallons. The business that is now the Finsbury Distillery was founded towards the peak of that boom, and no doubt in response to it.

Drink was becoming a substantial trade. The number of alehouses, selling beer, increased vastly, notably in the large towns to which people were flocking as a result of the industrial revolution. Licences to keep alehouses could be granted by any two justices of the peace, who did not even have to know the locality or the applicant. 'Taverns' were originally wine-houses, licensed by the king over the heads of the justices. From 1612, in an early charter of James I, freemen of the Vintners' Company were allowed the privilege of selling wine without licence within three miles of the City of London, in cities and port towns, and in the 'thoroughfare towns' on the major roads of England (for example, Leicester). From 1737 retailers of British wines and mead (that is, 'sweets') were required by law to be licensed victuallers.

So the company now known as the Finsbury Distillery derives directly from a business that was being managed at Holborn Bridge in the early 1740s by Robert Walsham, and was part of a growing and increasingly regulated trade. Having profited by the growth in trade, in 1744 or 1745 Walsham moved his business to Aldersgate Street, just outside London Wall, and at the end of the road that led north. Indeed, many of the coaches and carters began their journey from the Castle and Falcon Inn on Aldersgate Street.

Daniel Defoe described the expansion of London in the early years of the eighteenth century:

When I speak of London, you expect I shall take in all that vast mass of buildings, reaching from Black-Wall in the east, to Tot-hill Fields in the west; and extended in an unequal breadth, from the [London] bridge, or river [Thames], in the south, to Islington north; and from Peterburgh House on the bank side in Westminster, to Cavendish Square, and all the new buildings by, and beyond, Hannover Square by which the City of London, for so it is still to be called, is extended to Hide Park Corner in the Brentford Road, and almost to Maribone in the Acton Road, and how much farther it may spread, who knows? New squares, and new streets rising up every day to such a prodigy of buildings, that nothing in the world does, or ever did equal it, except old Rome in Trajan's time.[3]

Defoe also traced the northern boundary of expanding London as he knew it: from 'the west side of Gray's Inn Lane, going north [it] comes into the Islington Road by the Distiller's House, formerly Justice Fuller's. . . then turning north-west, passes by Sadler's Well'.[4]

There was good reason for distillers and brewers to settle in the northern periphery of London, and Sadler's Well is a reminder of it. The natural wells of north London provided a ready supply of clean water. In the seventeenth century, Islington Spa was known as 'New Tunbridge Wells' because of its health-giving waters; between there and the City of London were the London Spa near Exmouth Street, Bagnigge Wells, and the Clerks' Well. There the parish clerks of London used to meet once a year to perform a miracle play at St James's Church, as they had done since at least the twelfth century. In 1673 James, Earl of Northampton, as Lord of the Manor, presented the local spring and a plot of land for the use of the poor of the parish. It was leased by the vestry to John Crosse, a brewer.

There were two types of distillers in eighteenth-century

An easy freedom with a Cheerfull grace,
And tranquil Mind sits smiling in each face,
No busie envious talk about the State,
Nor 'gainst y Court nor Men in power prate;
I. Simon fecit et Excudit.

A
Winter Evenings
Conversation.

Each drinks his glass & wishes health to's friend,
His conversation and the Wine commend,
So long as they hold good content they stay,
Then friendly part to meet again next day.

A Winter Evening's Conversation depicts a convivial drinking party in a country house in about 1740, probably making a satirical allusion to Sir Robert Walpole's imminent retirement from office.

London. These were the malt distillers and the compound distillers. The first group distilled the raw spirit, mainly from corn. The second group were 'rectifiers', and had first been makers of cordials. Walsham was of the latter group (certainly his successors advertised themselves as such). The increasing number of London distillers in the early years of the eighteenth century is attributed to the prohibition of French brandy during the wars of the period. It was of course smuggled in – as Kipling wrote:

> Brandy for the Parson,
> 'Baccy for the Clerk[5]

– but was then too expensive for most people. Partly to provide a ready market for corn, in a period when the price of corn was dropping and the agricultural interests were suffering losses, legislation was passed to free the distillers. They were no longer bound by the charter of the Distillers' Company; from 1714 they were no longer required (like virtually all other trades) to serve a seven-year apprentice-ship; indeed on giving notice to the Excise Commissioners anyone was permitted to distil, and to retail spirits, without the need to be licensed by the justices.[6]

One result was great wealth for successful distillers. Lord Hervey asserted in Parliament in 1743 that

> the great fortunes recently made were to him a con-
> vincing proof that the trade of distilling was the most
> profitable of any now exercised in the kingdom except
> that of being broker to a prime-minister.[7]

Another result was profit for the farmers and landed gentry. But a third and tragic result was a vast increase in drunken-ness, mainly through gin-drinking, in London. In that period it was recorded that in Holborn one house in five was a gin-shop, where

> There enter the prude and the reprobate boy,
> The mother of grief and the daughter of joy,
> The serving-maid slim and the serving-man stout –
> They quickly steal in, and they slowly reel out.
>
> Surcharged with the venom, some walk forth erect,
> Apparently baffling its deadly effect;
> But, sooner or later, the reckoning arrives,
> And ninety-nine perish for one who survives.[8]

The magistrates at the petty sessions (who had to deal with the human tragedies in the streets) reported again and again on the scandal. The government of the day, aware of the revenues being recovered from the trade, was slow to

Hogarth's *Gin Lane* (1751) dramatizes the poverty, misery and degradation caused by the unrestricted sale of spirits. In the foreground of this scene, a street in St Giles's Westminster, lies an itinerant ballad-seller, who is said to have used the slogan 'Buy my ballads and I'll give you a glass of gin for nothing'.

act. Indeed, its first move was to attempt (in 1733) to introduce an Excise Bill that would levy taxes on tobacco and wine. In place of the old Customs regulations which taxed imported products at the point of entry to the country, it was now proposed to introduce bonded warehouses in which home-produced wines and spirits would be housed duty-free, to be released exclusively to licensed retailers on payment of an excise tax. There was a popular outcry, naturally fuelled by the distillers and gin-dispensers, and the Bill was withdrawn.

In 1736, however, the evidence of debauchery reported by the justices forced Sir Robert Walpole (First Commissioner of the Treasury) to attempt a measure of control. A duty of twenty shillings a gallon was to be levied on spirits, and retailers were required to take an annual licence costing the very considerable sum of £50. The measure failed, because it could not be enforced in the proliferating gin-shops. 'Prohibition' had not worked. By 1743 (the year after Walpole's departure from office), Parliament eventually passed an Act to try to reduce gin-drinking by stricter regulation, by increasing the price, and by limiting its consumption to licensed alehouses. Distillers were forbidden to retail. For a time this seemed to be working; then in 1747, claiming that they were suffering financial hardship, the distillers pleaded to be allowed to retail, and this was allowed on payment of a £5 licence.

Within a few years the terrible social conditions returned. In 1751 Parliament was once again obliged to legislate, and this time more firmly. Members of Parliament were made aware of the problem not only by petitions from the Corporation of London and from the London parishes, but by the publication of a pamphlet by the novelist Henry Fielding, *Reasons for the Late Increase of Robbers*, and, most potent of all, Hogarth's dramatic and devastating engraving *Gin Lane*. The duty on spirits was increased, and the places where it might be consumed were regulated. Distillers,

A Modern Contrast (1752) depicts the enforcement of the 1751 Excise Act. A caption in manuscript refers to a report that 'the spirituous liquors of a person in *Radcliffe-Highway* consisting of geneva, aniseed, plague-water, cinnamon and mint-water, cherry and raspberry brandy, in all amounting to upwards of 400 gallons, was turned down the channel, and the casks staved'.

chandlers and grocers were once again forbidden to retail: spirits had to be consumed at alehouses.

The distillers fought back with public relations. An engraving was published showing on one side of the street the Distillers' Arms, and on the other a public house at the sign of the Bear and Lamb, with the inscription 'Spirituous liquors sold here'. The distiller is being served with a writ, as his wife and children leave the house and his casks are being broken. The publican and his wife serve drinks and they boast that they abide by the law and are licensed. The figure of Justice with her sword and scales lies drunk on the ground.[9]

There is no evidence that distillers were driven into penury, and a few years later a commentator recorded that

> the lower people of late years have not drank spiritous liquors so freely as they did before the good regulations and qualifications for selling them. . . . The additional excise has raised their price, improvements in the distillery have rendered the home-made distillations as wholesome as the imported. We do not see the hundredth part of poor wretches drunk in the streets since the said qualifications as before.[10]

The population of London in the 1720s had been around 600,000. By the end of the century it was over 900,000, appreciably more sober and restrained in its drinking. This vast expansion of population was achieved, of course, by drawing in bright young people from the provinces who came to seek their fortune in a London whose streets, they believed, were paved with gold. Many of the sons of prosperous provincial families were sent to the metropolis. Most kept some association with their roots, and the most prosperous often used their wealth to endow schools and charities in the cities and towns where they had grown up. Others, if they themselves had no children, would summon their nephews from the home town to maintain the succession in London businesses.

Robert Walsham evidently profited from his distillery in Aldersgate Street, even with the restraints of 1751: no doubt he was one of those who ensured that his products were 'wholesome'. His business increased, so that in 1763 he took on a partner, John Bate, and the company became known as Walsham & Bate. Walsham's distinction in his trade is evidenced by his election in 1767 as Master of the Distillers' Company. By that time, indeed, his business was so successful that he was able to take on two young assistants – his elder son Thomas, and James Bishop. So the

Bishops return to the story once more.

James Bishop's branch of the family came from Leicester-shire, from the villages of Grimston and Asfordby, where they were people of some wealth and importance. Like so many country families, they gave their sons the same names in succeeding generations; the names of James, George and William recur. The Leicestershire family can be traced back to James Bishop (for clarity let us call him 'James I') who was a farmer in Grimston: he married Elizabeth Normanton in 1721 and they had at least two sons. James was born in 1723, and William two years later. The parents, with other Bishops of their generation, are buried in Grimston church-yard, to the east of the church on its windswept hill.

The elder son ('James II') became the leading member of the family locally in the late eighteenth century: Mayor of Leicester in 1782, Alderman, and landlord of the Three Crowns in Horsefair Street, its main entrance facing down Gallowtree Gate. The name of the hostelry commemorated the linking of the crowns of England, Scotland and Hanover in 1714 under King George I. Though given a Georgian stone facade with that new name, the original hostelry was evidently much older. Photographs taken when it was demolished a century ago show that at the back were medieval dormer windows. The hostelry was the most important in Leicester, for it was the place where the Royal Mail coaches from London to Sheffield stopped for the night. The Three Crowns enjoyed additional importance locally since it was from its balcony that election results were announced. Its landlord's family is commemorated in the name of Bishop Street nearby. Landlord James Bishop married: he and his wife Hannah have a memorial at St Margaret's Church, where they were buried.

The younger brother William ('William I') followed his father as a farmer and butcher in Grimston, where they cultivated 38 acres together with some other land at Asfordby nearby. He produced a large family, who became

The Three Crowns Inn, Leicester, of which James Bishop II and his nephew William Bishop II were both landlords. The photograph was taken in the nineteenth century, shortly before the building was demolished.

the beneficiaries of both brothers' wealth. It was one of William's sons, named James ('James III') after his uncle the landlord of the Three Crowns, who came to London in the 1760s and joined Robert Walsham in the distillery in Aldersgate Street. Nothing could have been more convenient; for when he went home to visit his family, he had only to walk a step or two from the distillery in Aldersgate Street to the Crown and Falcon Inn, and board the Mail coach, stepping out of it a day or two later at his uncle's inn at the centre of Leicester.

James learned from his master, prospered, and moved to a house in rural Hampstead. Eventually he felt his importance to be such that in 1810 he obtained a grant of arms.[11] He asked that they should be borne not only by his own descendants, but by his brother William Bishop ('William II') of Leicester (who had followed his uncle as landlord of the Three Crowns, and had also emulated him in local civic life, being Mayor of Leicester in 1799); by his younger brother Thomas Bishop, who had inherited the Grimston farm; by a third brother, Joseph Bishop, described as ('Merchant of London'); and by their only surviving sister, Sarah Bishop, who had remained un-married – perhaps because she acted as housekeeper for her uncle James after his retirement from the Three Crowns and the death of his wife. In his grant of arms, James III did not mention that there had been other brothers in the family. There was no need, in law, since they were dead by 1810; but one at least had offspring, who were not mentioned in the grant of arms.

The reason is revealed in the will of farmer William Bishop of Grimston, made in 1792, the year he died. He bequeathed his farm and estates to his young son Thomas (who was no doubt working them), or, failing him, to James (III) his successful son in London, or, failing him, to his friends John Simpson and Henry Gilbert. His other sons were not to get their hands on it:

Whereas I have bestowed upon my oldest son John Bishop a considerable sum of money for the purpose of settling him in business which through his indiscretion he has exhausted Now as token of my affection for him I do hereby give and bequeath unto my said Trustees . . . the sum of one hundred and sixty pounds upon Trust . . . & pay the interests and profits . . . unto my said son John Bishop.[12]

On his death, the interest was to be applied to the maintenance of his children. When landlord Alderman James (II) made his will in 1802, he left his niece Sarah (who was looking after him) his linen and silver, other silver to his nephew Thomas who was running the family farm, his gold watch to his successful London nephew James – and £200 on trust for his nephew John's children, their father having died. It would be fascinating to know whether it was in Leicester or London that the eldest son was settled in business; and, if in London, whether it was at the distillery. There is a further clause in the will that would have enabled the Trustees to help John more directly if he were to 'reclaim & become sober & attentive to business', but evidently he did not.

James III, on the other hand, proved an excellent man of business. In 1778 Robert Walsham retired, John Bate became senior partner and the company was named Bate & Walsham. For a time trade slumped, under the effects of heavy war taxes. But then in 1785 excise duty on British spirits was reduced and, within a few years, consumption (and therefore manufacture) doubled. The company prospered again, and James Bishop was well placed to make the best use of the greater opportunities.

In 1790 Bate died, and James Bishop became senior partner, together with Walsham's younger son Charles. However, because old Robert Walsham was still alive, the company name became Walsham & Bishop. On becoming senior partner, James Bishop began to plan his succession. He had no son. He married a Miss Scofield and was forty when their only child, a girl, was born. James III's younger brother William, now landlord of the Three Crowns in Leicester, had seven sons and six daughters by his two marriages. At least one of the sons could be spared to go and join his uncle's prosperous London business. Aged eighteen, George Bishop (third of the sons) travelled down to Aldersgate Street in 1803. It was a wise choice, because young George turned out to be not only a successful distiller and businessman, but also a notable scientist, a leading astronomer in the days when amateurs could rank with professionals in scholarship. His elder brother James joined him at the distillery later, but seems never to have achieved the multifarious successes of young George.

The Excise Act of 1751 having forbidden distillers to retail their products, they were obliged to make arrangements with others to sell their goods. From this date, the distillers had to create networks of sales outlets using the licensed public houses and retailers. Although 'grocers and chandlers' were also included in this prohibition, it is clear that this was applied to the consumption of spirits on the premises, and that grocers were permitted to sell bottles of spirits, for consumption 'off limits'.

When Robert Walsham's premises had been at Holborn Bridge, in the early 1740s, one of his neighbours and friends had been a successful grocer, John Stone of 230 High Holborn. It would, therefore, have been entirely reasonable for Walsham and his successors to enlist the services of their former neighbour. It also explains why the name that is associated with the principal product of the distillery – Stone's Original Green Ginger Wine – should not be that of the Bishop family, but of the retailer who was a principal agent.

There was a further matter that assisted British wine makers and 'rectifiers' in the last quarter of the eighteenth century. From 1789, the French Revolution threw that country into a ferment. In 1793 Britain declared war, to protect its supremacy in Europe. By 1795, however, the British Army had withdrawn from the continent, and the French threatened invasion. There was discontent in the British Fleet, and in 1797 there were mutinies in the Navy ships at Spithead and the Nore. But then matters righted themselves, helped by Nelson's victory that year at the

Battle of Cape St Vincent. The Royal Navy kept Britain's trade links open and, despite the ravages of Napoleon across Europe (indeed, partly because of them), William Pitt was able to tell Parliament in 1799 that 'our trade has never been in a more flourishing situation'.[13] The total value of foreign trade, £41.5 million in the year before the war, rose to £69 million in 1800.[14]

This was because the Navy kept the Baltic route open, and also the Atlantic (despite differences with the Americans over the searching of their ships on the high seas). As the cross-Channel trade with France declined, and the import of French wines and spirits fell away, the effects of this could only be helpful to the Bishop family's distillery (as it now effectively was) in Aldersgate Street. The value of wine imports (from all countries) did increase slightly between 1793, when the war began, to 1800 (£524,000 to £732,000). Then wine imports fell back in 1804 (to £459,000), only to rise sharply (to over £1 million) by 1808. There is evidence that the British distillers were making up the difference. The value of British spirits charged with duty for consumption had been over 8 million gallons in 1743 (the peak of the gin-drinking scandals), but had fallen back to under 2 million gallons by 1759, following the government's Acts to control and regulate consumption. Throughout much of the 1790s the volume was steady at about 4 million gallons. There was a sharp fall in 1797 to only 300,000 gallons; but by 1804 the dutiable production was 5.4 million gallons.[15]

It is therefore no coincidence that in 1804 James Bishop, as senior partner in the distillery, decided to look for larger premises. No doubt he was encouraged by the arrival of his nephew George from Leicester, adding to the business the strength and vigour of a new generation. He himself, now fifty-one, but with the inspiration and interest of a young daughter, a first child in his middle age, was thinking of retiring to his new estate at Stamford Hill.

They found a property not far away from Aldersgate, in

Finsbury. It occupied most of the area behind the houses in Finsbury Place, with a frontage to Ropemakers Street, and had the advantage that it was already a 'British Wine Manufactory', and is so described on the town maps. It had been built by Joseph and Richard James, who had operated it for at least twenty-five years, beginning as a cooperage business making wine casks, and then turning to the manufacture of wine. It needed minimal alteration for James Bishop and his nephew to begin distilling there, which they did in 1804, happy to be able to satisfy an increasing demand for spirituous liquors and wines. No doubt some of their increased production went to celebrate the great victory of Nelson at Trafalgar in October of the following year.

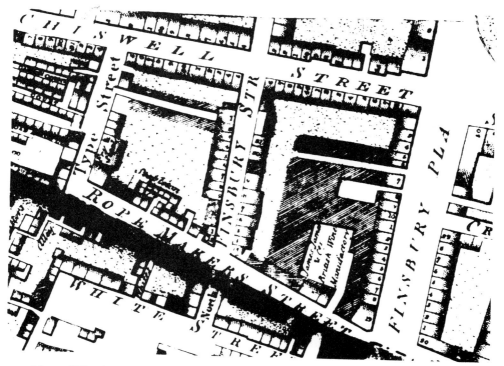

Map of Finsbury Place, showing the eventual site of the Distillery.

1873
Dec 12th

Gold Water
Acqua D'oro

26 lb Sugar	48/	.	12	..
3 liquor		..	..	..
3½ S. Wine 36	19/6	3	8	3
10 drops Oil Cearant		..	.	..
3 .. Oil Or peel		..	..	..
3 .. .. Cloves		..	.	..
5 oz Infusion Mace		..	2	6
6 .. .. Coriander		..	..	..
1/4 pint Orange flower water		..	..	..
1/2 drm Oil lemon		..	..	..
75 drops .. Saffron		..	..	..
		4	2 ..	9

7½ Gns
11/2

Silver water   Acqua D'argento
same as above
without Saffron

A nineteenth-century recipe from the Finsbury archives.

CHAPTER 2

Ropemakers Street

Some two years after the move to Ropemakers Street, James – brother of George Bishop – became a freeman of the Distillers' Company, by redemption (which meant that he did not take an apprenticeship, but paid £2 for the privilege), on 14 October 1806. On the same day, George Harrington also became a freeman. The Harrington family also had an interest in the Finsbury distillery. There is no very obvious reason why two years later George Harrington was admitted to the Livery of the Distillers' Company, while James Bishop did not choose to move forward in this way. George Bishop, the second brother, did not become a freeman of the Distillers' Company, doubtless because he was scarcely yet twenty-one.

The partners of the company in Ropemakers Street in the early years of the century were therefore James Bishop senior, Charles Walsham, and James Bishop's two nephews, James and George. By 1810 James Bishop, now living in Hampstead, was at the age of fifty-six a man of property and distinction. He therefore petitioned the Duke of Norfolk, Earl Marshal, for the grant of arms mentioned in the preceding chapter.

The arms are

Ermine a Cross patonce voided Gules in Chief two Roses of the last barbed and seeded Vert; and for the Crest On a Wreath of the Colours A Greyhound current Argent charged on the Body with a Cross patonce between two Roses Gules barbed and seeded Vert.

The reasons for these elements are unknown. The red roses with their thorns and green leaves have no obvious connection with the family. The unusual crest of the silver greyhound, running, may possibly be linked with the fact that the Three Crowns in Leicester adjoined the 'Bishop's Fee', an estate that had no connection with the Bishop family but belonged to the Bishop of Lincoln from at least 1088. It was then held by the Earl of Huntingdon and Northampton, and then by the Earls of Dysart, until the Corporation of Leicester purchased the fee simple of the 92 acres then remaining. There is, however, a racing association between St Margaret's Church, which the elder James Bishop attended and where he and his wife are buried and have memorials, and the Abbey Meadow associated with the 'Bishop's Fee': Leicester's town races were run in the meadow throughout the Middle Ages and until 1742. It may be that greyhounds were raced, too, and that the Bishop family was involved. (The coat of arms of Leicestershire County Council also has an animal as crest – the running fox, symbol of the hunting for which the county is renowned.) The motto, appropriately for this hard-working family, is *Labor Vincit Omnia*.

James Bishop senior subsequently moved to Stamford Hill in Middlesex with his wife Frances and daughter, also named Frances, who was born when her father was forty. He died in 1816, and among his bequests left his 'Scotch Encyclopaedia, Johnson's Dictionary and Williams's *Justice of the Peace* to his nephew George. The 'Scotch Encyclopaedia' would have been an early edition of the *Encyclopaedia Britannica*, first published in Edinburgh in 1768–71. The death of James Bishop marked a major change in the business. A public announcement in January 1817 indicated that Charles Walsham chose to retire, and the business would in future be carried on by James Bishop and George Bishop, with Thomas Harrington jun. The name of the

George Bishop FRS, 1784–1861.

company now changed to Bishop & Harrington, 'Rectifiers, Sweet-makers and Brandy-Merchants'.

'Sweets', in this definition, were sweetened cordials and wines (including the ginger wine that was soon to become a staple of the company). The company at this time divided its sales into three categories: British wines, Sweets, and Foreign wines. In 1816–17, the year when the Bishop sons succeeded their uncle as effective managing directors, they 'sent out' from Ropemakers Street nearly 190,000 gallons, of which 27,000 gallons were Foreign wines, 119,000 gallons were Sweets, and 44,000 gallons were British wines. The brothers set out to better this, and within the decade they had raised sales to nearly 300,000 gallons by 1825–6, of which much the greatest increase was in British wines. One memoir of George Bishop notes that 'the excise returns were said to exhibit half of all home-made wines as of his manufacture', and from the company's records this seems very likely.[1]

Certainly both the Bishop brothers felt confident enough of their future to marry at this time. James Bishop married Elizabeth Barcley, and in the summer of 1818 his younger brother George married Rosetta Houlditch at Hampstead. George Bishop chose as his home South Villa, in Regent's Park (the present Regent's College stands on the site).[2] There two sons were born – George jun. in 1825, and James jun. in 1830. That was not a good year for business: the output had dropped from nearly 300,000 gallons five years earlier to not much more than 200,000 gallons. But now the turn-round happened and, over the next decade and a half, sales rose to reach a peak of 390,000 gallons in 1847.

Various factors contributed to this. One, ironically, was the 'Beer Act' of 1830. Viscount Goulburn, Chancellor of the Exchequer in the Duke of Wellington's government, removed the tax on beer and cider. By the provisions of this curious Act, any ratepayer might open his house for the sale of beer, free from any control by the local justices, on payment of two guineas to the local excise office. Within six months, more than 24,000 new beer-houses had paid the fee and opened. In the previous years, the justices had regulated the standards of alehouses, and in order to improve them, the brewers had instituted the 'tied-house' system, providing landlords with finance in exchange for the exclusive sale of their products. In 1830 that changed.

One result was that many alehouses were transformed into taverns, selling wine and spirits. The House of Commons Committee on Drunkenness reported a few years later:

A low dirty public-house with only one doorway [would be converted] into a splendid edifice, the front ornamented with pilasters supporting a handsome cornice and entablature and balustrade, and the whole elevation remarkably striking and handsome. . . . The floor was sunk so as to be level with the street, and the doors and windows glazed with very large single squares of plate glass, and the gasfittings of the most costly description; the whole excited the surprise of the neighbourhood. . . . When this edifice was completed, notice was given by placards taken round the parish; a band of music was stationed in front. . . . The street became almost impassable from the number of people collected, and when the doors were opened the rush was tremendous; it was instantly filled with customers and continued so till midnight. . . . Many of the publicans have organs in their houses, and in Manchester, they played psalm tunes of Sunday evenings as an inducement for the parties to go and spend their money there rather than go to the beer shops.[3]

Such a gin-shop, recorded the Members of Parliament, was 'rising like a palace'. After all this redecoration, indeed, such houses came to be known as 'gin palaces'. Distillers

George Cruikshank produced several drawings of London gin shops in support of his own temperance campaign. This was one of twelve illustrations for the *Band of Hope Review* (1868).

like the Bishops vied to supply them with wines and spirits. It has to be remembered, as the Excise Commissioners reported in 1833, that 'the prevailing taste of principal consumers of spirits in England was still in favour of gin. . . . Whisky was practically unknown to the great body of English consumers at that period, the bulk of imports from Scotland and Ireland were corn-spirit for rectification and consumption as gin.'

The popularity of spirits over imported wine had been growing for a century and more. André Simon records that

> French wines became scarcer and dearer practically every year during the last decade of the seventeenth century; their consumption was more and more con-fined to a very small coterie of wealthy noblemen and extravagant men of letters, while spirits became more generally popular and the majority of wine drinkers gradually learned to resign themselves to Portuguese wines.[4]

Most of the foreign wine imported into England during the eighteenth century and the early years of the nineteenth came from Portugal, as a result of the Methuen Treaty, signed in 1703, which gave preferential treatment to the Portuguese. Gradually, even during the Napoleonic Wars, increasing quantities of French wines were imported. After the Methuen Treaty expired in 1831 and the duty on all imported wines were equalized, French wine imports challenged the Portuguese; but change was gradual and the sales of those two staples of the Finsbury Distillery, gin and British wines, continued to increase.

The sales of ginger wine also boomed, particularly in 1832. In that year there was a cholera epidemic, and within a few months more than 5000 died in London alone. It was believed that ginger wine had medicinal properties and would provide some protection against the disease, and not surprisingly the demand for ginger wine rocketed.

The popularity of British wines in general at this time is demonstrated by several recipe books that were published to encourage home wine-making. One of the most successful was first published in 1808 by John Davies, 'wine merchant', as *The Innkeeper and Butler's Guide, or a Directory in the Making and Managing of British Wines, together with Directions for the Managing, Colouring and Flavouring of Foreign Wines and Spirits, and to Making British Compounds, Peppermint, Aniseed, Shrub etc.*

Davies's list of British wines begins with 'English claret: 2 gallons cyder, 8 lbs raisins, juice of raspberries and black cherries and mustard seed'. Next is Frontignac Wine (elder-flower), English champagne (currants), English port (port, cyder, brandy, elderberries, sloes and cochineal), English mountain (raisins) and English sack (rue, fennel and honey). He also includes several recipes each for wines made from Raisin, Currant, Orange, Gooseberry, Pearl Gooseberry, Cowslip, Elderberry, Elder Flower, Damson, Cherry, Black Cherry, Strawberry, Raspberry and Cherry, Quince, Sage, Apricot, Balm, Mulberry, Blackberry, Ginger, Birch ('tap the tree for sap'), Lemon, and Clary (the last a plant of the Salvia family, and believed by apothecaries to be good for the eyes, thus 'clear-eye'). There is also a Wine of English Grapes.

His recipe for Ginger Wine is as follows (it bears some, but not very close, relation to the commercial product):

Take four gallons of water and seven pounds of sugar, boil them half an hour skimming it all the time. When the liquor is cold squeeze in the juice of two lemons; then boil the peels, with two ounces of white ginger, in three pints of water, one hour; when cold, put it altogether into the cask, with one gill of finings, and three pounds of Malaga raisins; then close it up, let it stand two months, and then bottle it off.

British Compounds included oil-based Peppermint, Caraway, 'Anniseed' and Wormwood. 'Usquebaugh', which to modern ears sounds very like whisky, adds 4 oz. liquorice to 3 gallons of spirits, with a formidable addition of 'cloves, mace, cinnamon, ginger, dates, raisins and saffron'. Other cordials were flavoured with Cloves, Cinnamon, Ratafia ('ambergris, peach and apricot kernels, and bitter almonds'), Coriander, Citron, and a dozen more, notably Imperial Nectar ('peach and apricot kernels, oil of orange, and herbs'), Queen's Cordial (mint) and Prince's Cordial ('cherry brandy and six pennyweights of the acid of vitriol'). The last sounds exceptionally nasty, and undoubtedly lethal.

A rival author some few years later, William Henry Roberts, in *The British Wine Maker*, published in Edinburgh in 1849, considered Davies's recipes 'ridiculous'. Perhaps in tribute to his home country, he derided the real Ginger Wine in favour of a concoction that can only be read as an excuse to produce spirits lightly flavoured with ginger. In so doing, he drew a distinction that has often been held against ginger wine, but he also pays tribute to its popularity:

> What is called ginger wine has, of late years, come into very general use. The term is, however, misapplied. That which usually goes by this name is a mere compound of water, spirits, fruits and spices; for no liquor ought to be called wine that is not really fermented; and fermentation is never really attempted in forming this mixture, which is in fact nothing else than a very strong, rich punch.
>
> I had a conversation recently with a person who makes and sells a great quantity of this unfermented compound, or punch, known by the name of Ginger Cordial. I asked him how much spirit he generally used to the gallon? He replied that he was in the habit of putting two bottles of whisky in each gallon; but as he found complaints made by his customers of its want of strength, he was obliged to increase the dose. . . .

This Ginger Cordial, claimed Roberts, 'has obtained such repute that in the mansion and in the cottage it is alike to be found. From almost every wine-merchant, grocer and spirit-dealer in Scotland, it may be purchased. Indeed, so great is the consumption of it, that hundreds of dozens are sent from Leith to London monthly'. That may have been so; but the production of Bishop and Harrington's (later to be Stone's) Original Green Ginger Wine – which had always been a fermented product – exceeded these quantities, and London and the home counties stayed loyal to the local wine.

The name of the firm changed again in the 1830s. Thomas Harrington jun. retired in 1835; George Bishop had been left alone in the partnership at just that time by the death of his brother James. George therefore took Bennett Pell into the partnership, which from 1836 became Bishop & Pell. Bennett Pell belonged to a leading family of City merchants and sugar refiners, with particular associations with the brandy trade. He had invested appreciable sums in the Bishops' business for the previous twenty years; in 1833 his share was reckoned at over £10,000, and by 1846 had risen to over £52,000. Pell was therefore an important asset to the firm.

In the eighteenth century it had not been unusual for rich men to take an interest in academic work. The development of the natural sciences was often considerably advanced by amateurs. They took the trouble to find out the experts in their field of interest, and to invest the money they had made in industry in the pursuit of scholarship. George Bishop did precisely this.

The Astronomical Society of London had been founded in London in 1820. Two of its distinguished founders were John Herschel, son of one of the greatest eighteenth-century astronomers, and Charles Babbage, now honoured as the 'inventor' of the computer. George Bishop became interested in the society's work in its early years, and was

George Bishop's observatory in his garden in Inner Circle, Regent's Park, 1836.

elected to membership in 1830. He was modest enough to recognise his own deficiencies, and took lessons in algebra in order to understand the mathematical theories that underlie observations in astronomy. In 1836 he built a small observatory in his garden in Regent's Park (subsequently to be the site of Bedford College in the University of London, and now of Regent's College). He soon became a valued colleague of the leading astronomers of the day, and was secretary of the Astronomical Society from 1833–9, and honorary treasurer for the formidable period of seventeen years, from 1840–57.

As his memorialist in the *Dictionary of National Biography* comments:

> No expense was spared in [his observatory's] equipment, and the excellence of the equatorial furnished by Dollond (aperture, seven inches) confirmed his resolve that some higher purpose than mere amusement should be served by the establishment. 'I am determined,' he said when choosing its site, 'that this observatory shall do something'. The Rev. William Dawes conducted his noted investigations of double stars at South Villa 1839–44; Mr John Russell Hind began his memorable career there in October of the latter year.

Hind was awarded the Gold Medal of the Astronomical Society in 1853, and Dawes in 1855.

In 1847 the Astronomical Society was involved in a complicated dispute of the kind peculiar to academics. There had been one remarkable astronomical discovery during the year, the discovery of the planet Astraea. But there was great argument as to whether the prize for its discovery should go to a French astronomer, to a Cambridge scholar, or to that year's President of the Astronomical Society. As a way out of this impasse, the society decided not to award its Gold Medal that year, but instead to award twelve Testimonials to scholars who had done good work, including the three contending Astraea scholars. One of the recipients of a Testimonial was George Bishop, then honorary treasurer of the society, 'for the foundation of an observatory leading to various astronomical discoveries'. This is evidence of the respect in which George Bishop was held by his contemporaries (even if there was considerable criticism of the fact that the officers of the Astronomical Society had voted Testimonials to themselves). George Bishop was elected President of the [Royal] Astronomical Society in 1857 and 1858, but unfortunately was beginning to suffer from physical illness, and was never able to chair a meeting.

> His character, both social and commercial, was of the highest, and his discriminating patronage of science raised him to the front rank of amateurs. He was elected a Fellow of the Royal Society 9 June 1848, was also a Fellow of the Society of Arts, and sat for some years on the council of University College.[5]

The year 1848 was a year of revolution in Europe, and there were many who believed that revolutionary fervour might take root in Britain too. It did not.

For George Bishop and the family company, it was a year of triumphant success, probably the greatest sales year that Finsbury had ever achieved. Nearly 400,000 gallons were sent out of the manufactory, considerably beating the previous record of 300,000 gallons achieved twenty years earlier. The sales of imported or Foreign wines were still around 20,000 gallons and so made only a minor contribution to the sales. British wines showed a small decline, and were running around 140,000 gallons. But there was a huge increase in the sales of Sweets, or sweetened cordials (including Ginger Wine), which rose by steady progression over four years from 140,000 gallons a year to 240,000 gallons.

On 30 June 1848 Bennett Pell retired from the partnership. He was a Liveryman of the Distillers' Company, but had only become a freeman in 1841 ('by redemption': he paid £3). The reason may be found in the Distillers' Company records for the following year, when on 11 October he took two apprentices into the Finsbury business, Bennett Pell (jun.) and Paul Pell. Perhaps they were his twin sons; but, for whatever reason, neither seems to have completed his apprenticeship and there is no further record of them working in the business. Evidently Bennett Pell (sen.) died soon after leaving the partnership (perhaps illness was the reason for his departure), for later that year the firm paid his executors nearly £46,000.

With business booming, George Bishop was faced with a personnel crisis. His brother James had died twelve years earlier (and George and his wife had adopted his young daughter Emily Ann, bringing her up as their own). Now his partner was leaving the business. George Bishop was keen to spend more of his time on his scholarly interests in astronomy, and not be saddled constantly with the over-seeing of the family business. He urgently needed more help.

His sons were growing up. The elder, George, now twenty-three, had married the previous summer – Clara, the daughter of Samuel Norman Cowley. The younger son, James, was only seventeen – but his father had not been much older when he had come down from Leicester to join the business, and so was no doubt sympathetic to his younger son also starting work at that age. He may well have astutely recognised that it was the younger son who would make the more serious contribution to the business.

A partnership indenture was therefore drawn up and signed by George Bishop and his two sons on 3 July 1848. It is a document of quite remarkable detail. It asserts that the agreement is being made 'in consideration of the natural love and affection which he hath and beareth towards his Sons George Bishop the younger and James Bishop.' Never-theless it makes totally clear that George Bishop was to have the ruling hand over the business, and that he could terminate the agreement at any time. The business was valued at £90,000. The profits for the first year were to be divided among the partners so that the father would receive

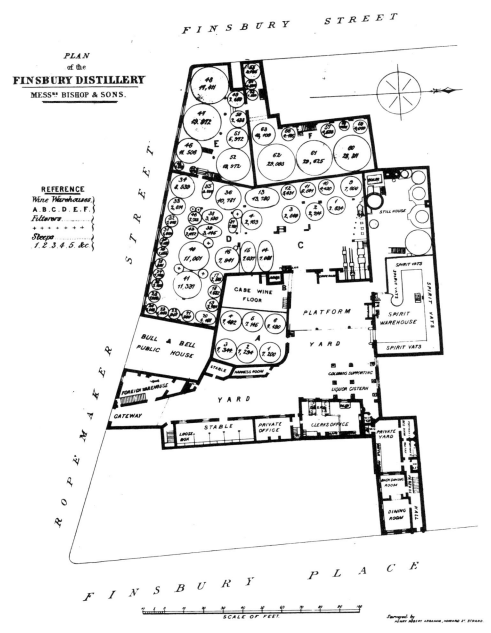

Plan of the Finsbury Distillery in Ropemakers Street, *c.* 1850.

70 per cent, the younger George Bishop 25 per cent, and the seventeen-year-old James Bishop 5 per cent. For the second and subsequent years the profits were to be divided into four, George Bishop the elder to receive two fourths, and each of his sons one fourth. The name of the business was to become 'Bishop & Sons'.

A year and seven days after that indenture was signed, young James Bishop felt confident enough about his future to marry (at the age of eighteen). It was a good match, since Isabella Marson, whom he married at St Marylebone parish church, was the daughter of a successful and wealthy London solicitor, Thomas Frederick Marson, whose firm subsequently acted for the Finsbury Distillery.

The business continued to thrive, and by 1851 George Bishop senior's capital was valued at £102,484, that of his son George at £6143 and of his son James at £4144. The partnership books indicate that there were other investors in the company, mainly relatives of the Bishop family, among them Sarah Baker (who was George Bishop senior's sister) but also including Bennett Pell jun. (who invested £16,000) and George Bishop's brother-in-law Captain Philip Gostling, who was married to Bishop's sister Anne (£5000). The books demonstrate that in 1851 over £10,000 of the firm's annual profit was added to the capital of the company.

In 1853 a significant name appears in the trading registers of 'Sweets sent out' of the factory. It is noted that in August and September, 'Stone exchanged 1,140 and 1,282 gallons'. So the name that has become synonymous with ginger wine enters the story.

CHAPTER 3

The Original Mr Stone

Joseph Stone had begun to work for the Bishop family at Ropemakers Street in about 1826, when he was seventeen years old. That was a prosperous year for the business, with production expanding, and evidently Joseph Stone was one of the extra hands taken on to cope with the workload. The Stone family was as long-established in the London wine trade as the Bishops. In the mid-eighteenth century, at the same time as Bishops were trading as distillers in High Holborn, John Stone (as we have already learnt) was in business as a grocer and tea dealer at 230 High Holborn (tea was then, of course, a newly fashionable drink, brought to Britain by voyagers to the East). But grocers were also retailers of wines and spirits. So there were solid reasons for an association between the grocer and the distiller, since the first provided the retail outlet for the products of the second.

John Stone the grocer had fifteen children, of whom Joseph was the thirteenth child and seventh son.[1] It was therefore a bonus that he could place his son in so prosperous an employment as the Finsbury Distillery of Bishop & Harrington. For his part, young Joseph set himself thoroughly to learn the business, and he came to specialize in the sales side. He then married. His wife, whom he met at the chapel they both attended at Bunhill Fields, was Sarah Lee Hale. She had been orphaned at an early age, but she was blessed with two formidable and supportive brothers – Ford Hale, who was a wax chandler (candle-

Joseph Stone, 1809–1896.

maker) in Cannon Street, and his younger brother Warren Storms Hale, whom he had taken into apprenticeship.

Warren Storms Hale became hugely successful, largely by adopting and introducing to his family business various new discoveries by French chemists concerning the properties of animal and vegetable fats (an admirable instance of an industrialist looking out for, and being willing to introduce, new technologies). Having made his fortune in business, Warren Storms Hale began to enter public life in the City. As Chairman of the City Lands Committee, he determined that the City should create a day school for boys, and that it should provide a sound academic education. Warren Storms Hale achieved this aim: the City of London School, though based on earlier foundations, was established by Act of Parliament in 1834, and Warren Storms Hale was and is honoured as its 'second founder'.

By 1848, the year of the great change at the Distillery when Bennett Pell retired and the two Bishop sons joined the partnership, Joseph Stone had left the direct employ of the business and began to deal on his own account as a wine and spirit merchant at 61 Crown Street, Finsbury. This was not far from the Bishops' premises, and it is clear that his departure was friendly, and that he and the Bishops were mutually able to extend the business by capitalizing on the particular association he had established with retail wine merchants. Soon he moved his business even nearer to the Distillery, with an establishment at 27 Finsbury Place.

Meanwhile his brother-in-law Warren Storms Hale was Lord Mayor of London in 1864–5. He could seem a little rough-and-ready, 'only a tallow-chandler . . . one who had lived and worked amongst his men, and was not ashamed that everyone should know it. I fear [wrote a former pupil of the school in later years] the snobbishness of boys did not fully see the man behind the tallow; but still we did like and respect him, as we had good reason to do.'[2]

Indeed, as Lord Mayor he threw an evening party for the

school at the Mansion House in February 1865; it seems to have been a notable occasion, attended by 671 boys.

> The venerable Lord Mayor mingling, like our kind headmaster, with the crowd of happy boys, seemed to delight in their delights. . . . The Coldstream Band played lively airs. . . . After nine, supper was announced on the first floor, and the provident immediately proceeded thither fearing the rush that came in time. Batch after batch went up, batch after batch came down, chanting the charms of champagne and the chicken, singing the savour of the salad, bepraising the boar's head, and lauding the Lord Mayor as a (hiccup) brick. . . . Others executed to perfection the strain of 'We won't go home till morning' in the Drawing-room, certain distinguished members of the 5th [form] leading the tuneful choir.

Fortunately for the structure of the Mansion House, the revellers had left by 11 o'clock, 'most to bed', writes the chronicler.[3] The occasion is ample evidence of the character of Warren Storms Hale. Unfortunately no record survives to indicate whether some or all of the liquors consumed that evening were supplied by the Finsbury Distillery or Joseph Stone.

Certainly by this time the Distillery had been supplying Stone with wines and cordials on an 'own name' basis; and the labels, in the familiar dark pine green, carry the City of London coat of arms and motto, *Domine Dirige Nos*. The Bishop business itself at this time sold its product as 'Bishop & Pell's Original Green Ginger Wine', on a label of the same green, but without the City of London arms. It may reasonably be deduced that Joseph Stone introduced the City reference with the authority of – or perhaps as a tribute to – his brother-in-law as he moved from one distinction to another in the City – Deputy of Coleman

Label used by Bishop & Pell.

Street Ward, Alderman, Sheriff, and then Lord Mayor.

His 'own name' brands continued to be increasingly successful in the trade, and therefore the name Stone became familiar. But Bishop & Sons maintained their name for spirits and liqueurs. In these years they were distilling 'Strong Gin', 'British Hollands' and 'British Brandy', and many varieties of cordials and liqueurs including Best Rum Shrub ('Shrub' was a prepared drink, particularly popular in the eighteenth century, made from orange or lemon juice, sugar, and rum), Common Rum Shrub, Mint, Punch with Brandy, Lovage, Maraschino, Foreign Cherry, Copenhagen Cherry ('Morella'), Noyeau, Doctor and Crème de Thé. The recipe for Doctor includes cloves, ginger brandy, and bitters; and Crème de Thé contained black tea, green tea, and 'liquor'.

A formidable recipe survives headed 'Punch (Mr Geo Bishop)', and is sufficient for 38 gallons:

> Parings 20 lemons
>> Do. 20 Seville oranges

Put into 10 Gallons Rum, Stand 4 days, then take 20 Gallons liquor, and 60 lbs lump sugar boiled, with the whites of 60 eggs added when it boils.

When cold strain through sieve, and pour the Rum from the parings into Syrup, add 10 quarts Orange juice, and 6 quarts Lemon juice, also strained.

			l	s	d
20 lemons		1½		2	6
20 oranges		1½		2	6
10 Rum		13/2	6	11	8
60 eggs		1d		5	0
10 qts or juice	4 gs	1/-		4	0
6 qts lem juice)					
1/4 or. flower water					
60 lbs sugar			1	5	0
			8	10	8

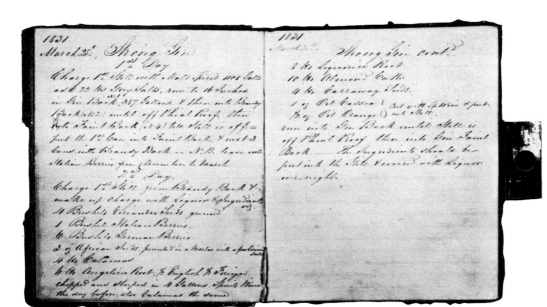

An entry from the secret recipe book.

George Bishop, the elder son, remained childless; but his younger brother James soon started a family. His eldest son George Frederick was born in March 1852, a daughter Emily in November 1852, a second son William Henry in February 1855, and a third son Charles Willoughby in August 1859. George became increasingly interested in his father's astronomical research, and less interested in the business. It is clear from the partnership ledgers that James Bishop was deliberately increasing his capital in the business, while his elder brother George was reducing his.

George Bishop sen. died at South Villa, Regent's Park, on 14 June 1861. The sum of £128,311 was removed from the company's capital for probate; the capital remaining to the sons was £1434 to George and £17,198 to James. By his will, after making generous provision for his widow Rosetta, the elder George left his estate in equal shares to his two sons. He left his property at Leicester to them also; but he gave his 'share and interest in the London University College' specifically to James, presumably since he had sons who might be educated there.

The departure of George Bishop sen. occurred at a particularly important time for the wine trade. In the previous year, 1860, the Chancellor of the Exchequer had used his first budget of a new administration to revise the system of taxation of wines. The Chancellor was William Ewart Gladstone. He explained his reasons, and in passing made a pleasant reference to 'highly respectable manufacturers' of British wines, among whom the Bishops were certainly numbered.

While the consumption of foreign wines has fallen from 6,225,000 gallons to 5,893,000 gallons, there has been an increase in the manufacture of British wines. . . . In the hands of the highly respectable manufacturers, and I am not referring at all to what is sold for fraudulent purposes, [British wine] is made very much with raisins, sugar and brandy. The duty paid on these materials is reckoned as amounting to 1s 2d a gallon. Therefore you have a duty on foreign wines of 5s 10d, on colonial wines [mainly, at that time, from 'the Cape', as South Africa was called] of 2s 10d, and on British wines of 1s 2d. The result is that the consumption of colonial wines had increased; and the consumption of British wines has doubled within the last ten years.[4]

As the result of a commercial treaty negotiated by Richard Cobden with the French, its main purpose being to encourage British exports to France, the wine duty was cut markedly, the duty on wine being set in two classes, that not exceeding 26 degrees of proof spirit, and that exceeding that level. The result was to free the market for the import of (specifically) French wines. Within a decade the import of foreign wines increased from an average of under 9 million gallons a year to over 14 million; the import of French wine increased in the same period from 743,000 gallons a year to over 3 million gallons.

Although much of these large quantities was imported by merchants to be laid down, rather than immediately consumed, the result was to transform the British wine trade. As Gladstone had intended, it diminished (if it did not entirely bring to an end) the practices of 'fraud and adulteration'.

Many of the gentlemen engaged in the wine trade bear as high a character as any in England [said Gladstone]. But those gentlemen will tell you of the difficulties they have to encounter in holding their ground against persons of inferior character who are brought into the trade . . . because our law invites them. The restrictive operation of your tariff is so severe that it affords temptations to counterfeit the articles on which you have laid such heavy duties.[5]

Some years later Gladstone was able to look back and claim, with reason, that as the result of his cuts in duties

> great progress has been made in facilitating the consumption of wine, cheap wine, and of sound wine throughout the country. That character of the trade has been fundamentally changed – adulteration is greatly diminished, and the consumption of sound wine and cheap wine has been very greatly increased.[6]

Naturally the increased import of wines led to an increase in the number of retailers, many of whom introduced their own brand names. Marketing became much more important, and it was necessary to defend the sale of British wines against the threat posed by the increase in the import of wine from abroad.

Recognising this, George and James Bishop decided to change the relationship between their company and Joseph Stone. Joseph was at this time fifty-two, and no doubt considering retirement. On 21 August 1861, he signed a Deed of Arrangement with George and James Bishop. It read in part:

> Whereas . . . Joseph Stone has for several years purchased of the said firm of Bishop & Sons British Wines manufactured by them and has sold the same under his own name and labelled. . . . It has been agreed between the parties hereto that the said Joseph Stone shall from and after the twentyninth day of September next relinquish the sale of British wines on his own account and shall then undertake the duties of a Traveller for the purpose of promoting the sales of British Wines solely on account of them the said George Bishop and James Bishop. . . .

A similar arrangement covered the sales of Foreign wines.

The advantage to each side is evident from the clause that

George Bishop and James Bishop their executors ad-
ministrators and assigns shall at all times hereafter
have the exclusive right to use the name of . . . Joseph
Stone and the labels . . . in order to promote their sale of
British wines.

The Bishops were to pay to Joseph Stone £200 a year, and in
addition

a commission of Four Pence per Gallon on all British
wines sold by them within the London District.

Joseph Stone would 'provide his own horses and con-
veyances and shall bear all other expenses of travelling'. He
would have needed them, for the 'London District' was
defined in a schedule attached to the agreement as being
most of south-east England. It comprised the whole of
the modern 'Greater London', and then north as far as
Hendon and Stanmore, east (north of the river) to Ilford and
(south of the river) to Rochester, Chatham and Sheerness. In
the south it took in Croydon and Leatherhead, and in the
west to Hounslow and Windsor. It was a very lucrative
agreement and, while initially contracted for ten years,
lasted a great deal longer. A note in the partnership books
indicates that Joseph Stone's commission on sales in the
year 1862 was £107, which in addition to his fee would
have provided an annual income of something over £18,000
a year (1980s prices). This was enough to enable him
eventually to retire to a new home at Barnet where he
involved himself with the affairs of the local chapel. There
he died in 1896; no doubt a modest man, he would be much
surprised to know that, nearly a century later, his name still
resounds through the wine trade and in many countries of
the world.

Trademarks and Taverns

When James Bishop succeeded to the control of the business on his father's death in 1861, he had every incentive to make a success of it. With three small sons and a daughter, he had a family to provide for. But, while still a young man, he had worked at Ropemakers Street for eight years and was fully in charge. His brother George, five years older, inherited the big family house in Regent's Park with its observatory in the grounds. Married but childless, he decided that he would move to Meadowbank, Twickenham, and had the observatory transferred there so that he could continue his father's scientific work.

James and his wife moved out of South Villa with their young family to a smaller house nearby in Park Square East, Regent's Park. It was no doubt significant that James continued to live within reasonable distance from his work in Ropemakers Street, while George moved out to the salubrious suburbs. During 1862 there was much discussion about the precise state of the accounts of the company; the difficulty was not over its prosperity or profitability, admirable on both counts, but over the division between the partners. By 1863, after a major reorganisation of the books conducted by the solicitor Frederick Marson (who happened to be James Bishop's father-in-law), it was agreed that the capital in the company due to George Bishop was £41,421 4s. 5d., and to James Bishop £75,242 8s. 2d. This was a direct acknowledgement of James's controlling interest.

By 1869 George Bishop (now in his mid-forties) wanted

to divest himself of even nominal responsibility for the day-to-day management, and the brother signed an agreement whereby James would be in full executive control and George would become merely a sleeping partner. The arrangement also defined the terms under which the partners might introduce sons into the business – something that was of keen concern to James, with his three sons, and less so to George, who remained childless. For whatever reason, George required a clause to be written into the agreement that partners would be expelled if found guilty of 'gambling or any disreputable conduct' (which the lawyers translated as 'gambling or any conduct calculated to bring the business into disrepute'). One wonders whether some rash boyish escapade on the part of one of James's young sons (at this time seventeen, fourteen and ten) brought on this access of puritanism on the part of the elder brother. The clause was written into the agreement, and only removed some years later.

In 1869 George Bishop not only left the business, but also left the country, taking up residence with his wife Clara in the South of France at the Château de Barla, outside Nice. There they joined the fashionable society world of British expatriates, living on the steadily expanding profits of successful British industrial growth. George Bishop's particular pleasure was his yacht *Pearl*, in which he cruised in the Mediterranean. His wife Clara died in Naples in 1875, and thereafter George married again – Caroline Felicité Davis of Carthage. He died at the Château de Barla in October 1883. Although he left his widow an annuity of £3000 a year there was not sufficient capital to provide this, and despite a generous offer by James to pay his sister-in-law, she at first refused this since she did not feel entitled to it.

By this time James Bishop's two elder sons had joined their father in Ropemakers Street: George Frederick Bishop became a partner in 1876 (when he was twenty-four) and William Henry Bishop in 1890 (aged thirty-five). Their younger brother, Charles Willoughby Bishop, when he came of age, did not join the business but (like so many younger sons of wealthy families) became a regular soldier, finishing as a Major in the 9th Lancers. He married (in 1896) the daughter of an Irish landowner and politician, Henry Bruen, a former Member of Parliament, Privy Councillor, and Deputy Lieutenant and High Sheriff of County Carlow. Though Charles Willoughby Bishop did not join the business, his son Geoffrey Charles Bishop (also an officer in the 9th Lancers) became a director, as also, briefly, did his grandson Charles Julian Bishop.

There was another Bishop family connection with Ireland, since in 1878 James's eldest son George Frederick married (in Dublin) Margaret Josephine Wilson, the daughter of an Irish merchant with business in Trinidad. Their first child, a daughter (Sibyl) was born at their house in Upper Berkeley Street, London, in 1880. Five years later their elder son, Gerald Herbert, was born; he was followed two years afterwards by another son, named Algernon Charles.

Through the 1860s and 1870s the company continued to prosper, making a regular and substantial profit, but not markedly increasing its sales. In fact, through these two decades, production (at least of Sweets, for which the records survive) tended to decline, faced with the challenge of the imports of cheap foreign wines as a result of the cuts in duty introduced by Gladstone in his 1860 budget. In 1869 the number of gallons 'sent out' from Ropemakers Street was 158,423, while by 1886 this had declined to 105,619. One of the greatest innovations in this period was the sale of wines and cordials in bulk to other merchants: from the 1850s the names of Lamb, Lamb & Watt, Cutler Palmer, and Berry begin to appear as substantial purchasers of the distillery's products. In the 1870s the firm of Lamb were buying annually over 16,000 gallons of Sweets from Ropemakers Street.

Another innovation, in 1875, was the introduction of

registered trade marks and from this year the range of trade marks and labels used by the Finsbury Distillery on its own account and in association with Joseph Stone was formally on the record. The other innovation, in 1882, was the introduction to the sales list of an own brand whisky, named Rothsay. This was blended in Ropemakers Street from a number of whiskies bought in Scotland. It no doubt presaged the decision of the Bishop family to develop particular associations with public houses, since with an own brand of Scotch whisky added to the London gin already being distilled in-house, the company was well placed to build up its own group of retail outlets. Whisky

A Stone's advertisement on a London omnibus, 1893.

was at this time beginning to challenge gin as the most popular spirit. Though hardly sold in London earlier in the century, it had taken the sales lead from gin by 1900. The success of whisky (not only Scotch, but Irish whiskey also began to be sold in London from the mid-1860s) was also helped by the failure of brandy: the scourge of phylloxera in the European vineyards meant that virtually no brandy was distilled in the 1880s.

By chance, the company's move towards developing links with specific retail outlets (the tied house had been customary among the brewers throughout the century) seems to have been planned in the year of Queen Victoria's Golden Jubilee, 1887, and implemented in the following year. The main bulk product to sustain this development was known initially as 'cheap wine', but this name was swiftly replaced by 'draught wine'. This was wine supplied in casks to the public houses – mainly in the London area – being taken over by the company, by lease or purchase. At one period 273 pubs were either owned or leased by the Finsbury Distillery. The success of this operation is demonstrated by the despatch statistics.

Year	Total Sales (gallons)	Sales of draught wine (gallons)
1890	212,515	102,188
1891	252,356	132,373
1892	309,199	194,882
1893	332,303	222,963
1894	313,948	210,667

The books show that a keen eye was kept on the performance of the houses in which Finsbury had an interest. Of the Spread Eagle in Mortimer Street, W, it is noted that 'more trade could be done here: advise letter in strong terms'. The North Pole, in St Mary Street, Woolwich, 'should pay more than it does'. The Odell Arms in Chelsea 'must increase payments and trade'. The landlord of the Red Lion in St George's Street, EC, 'is dealing elsewhere: should purchase all he requires through us'.

Evidently Finsbury would provide loans to landlords whose tenancies were from other sources; naturally they would then favour Finsbury. The landlord of the Duke of Wurtemburg in Stamford Street in 1897 is recorded as having a yearly tenancy from Barclays at a rent of £120. Finsbury had lent him £150, to be paid off at £15 a month (though the sharp eye at Finsbury noted that 'this man can pay £35 and should be judiciously coerced'). At whatever rate, he paid off the loan within two years. There is a note that the pub was sold (presumably by Barclays, and one hopes at a profit to everyone including the landlord) in June 1900.

In those public houses owned or leased by the Finsbury distillery, their own products would be presented in miniature varnished wooden casks placed on the counter or the shelves behind. In 1892, an advertisement announced that 'Stone's Ginger Wine is on draught at all First-class Taverns, Refreshment Bars, and Confectioners: Sold in bottles by Grocers, Wine Merchants & Stores everywhere.' The pubs, with the products advertised in engraved glass mirrors, were in themselves the most vigorous advertisement. But additionally, the main public advertising was on hoardings and on the mobile billboards provided by omnibuses; there are many photographs of London in the 1890s with 'Stone's Ginger Wine' prominent on the sides of vehicles.

For seven years after George Bishop died (in 1883) James Bishop was the senior partner, with his eldest son as junior partner (from 1876). Then in 1890 he decided to bring his younger son into partnership. At this time he believed that William Henry Bishop was still unmarried at thirty-five. In fact he had married, but secretly, since his wife was a Catholic and, because of that, unacceptable to his father. The marriage produced two sons, Harry and Geoffrey, who initially took their mother's name of Burns. William Bishop looked after their education (they were sent to Downside, one of the leading Catholic public schools), and Harry was eventually to join the business.

One purpose of the 1890 family arrangement was to look after George Bishop's widow by paying her an annuity of £1200; the partnership would also pay her interest on its profits, presumably in respect of money left by her in the business. Another participant in the agreement was Richard Cowley Tyllier Blunt 'of Château Barla, retired Lieutenant in the Royal Navy'. As George Bishop's first wife's maiden name was Cowley, it may be assumed that he was a relative.

By 1890 James Bishop had found himself a substantial country estate – Hamstead Park, at Newbury in Berkshire. He continued to be a most active senior partner in the business; and after the death of his eldest son George Frederick Bishop in February 1898 (at the age of forty-five) James rearranged the partnership so that George Frederick's two sons, Gerald Herbert Bishop and Algernon Charles Bishop, might inherit their father's share on old James's death, should they reach the age of twenty-one.

Stone's commemorative blotter, 1896.

STONE'S GINGER WINE

STONE'S GINGER WINE is on draught at all First-class Taverns, Refreshment Bars, and Confectioners.
SOLD IN BOTTLES BY GROCERS, WINE MERCHANTS & STORES EVERYWHERE.

Advertisement from *The Graphic*, 7 January 1893.

Turn-of-the-century advertising on a London omnibus.

A Finsbury Gin mirror from the public houses that
at one time formed part of the business.

An advertising poster for Rothsay whisky, showing an artist's impression of the new Moreland Street premises in 1904.

The bustard shot by Algernon Bishop on the Williams estate in Spain: it now welcomes visitors to the Finsbury Distillery.

The 'small' certificate (approximately 1ft 9ins × 2ft 6ins), marking the award to Finsbury of a silver medal in the Brewers' Exhibition competition of 1907, for Ruby Wine at over 27% alcohol.

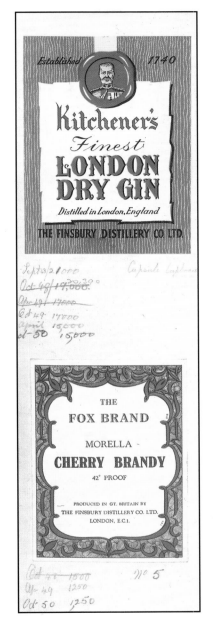

This page and overleaf: A selection of labels used by Finsbury over the years: the quantities for some of the orders are also shown.

The 1950s party book, including entertainment such as 'The Bottle Dance' and 'Goofy Golf'.

The 1987 *Winter Report* which contained such momentous news as '17% more women use antifreeze than men'!

Some of the range of Stone's Ginger products, with examples of bottles
from the main export markets of Australia, Jamaica, New Zealand and
Canada.

CHAPTER 5

To Moreland Street

*B*y the beginning of the new century, the premises in
Ropemakers Street were far too small to contain the
growing business of the Finsbury Distillery. In addition,
there was another powerful incentive to move. The buildings in Ropemakers Street were so cramped that there was
no practicable way in which the company could conform
precisely to legislation introduced in the 1880s governing
the layout of rectifying premises. The old buildings did
not allow these activities to be strictly segregated from
wine-making. The Inland Revenue had granted a 'special
indulgence' allowing the business to continue for a limited
period; it had carried on for a decade, but sooner or later the
regulations would be enforced.

So it was essential for a move to be made, despite the
difficulties. These were very real, not least the problems of
moving the huge vats that had stood in Ropemakers Street
for nearly a hundred years. They dated from the days when
wine-makers believed that wines matured more quickly in
large quantities. Several of these vats held more than 20,000
gallons; one, with a capacity of 28,902 gallons, was larger
than the famous 'tun of Heidelberg' (which is in the Castle
ruins, and has a stairway to the top, even though it is lying
on its side). The 'tun of Finsbury' was no tourist attraction,
but a wholly practical wine-vat – and said then to be the
biggest vat in Europe.

After considering various sites, the partners decided to
move just one mile to the north-west, where they leased

land from the Marquis of Northampton's Estate on the corner of Moreland Street and Central Street. It was convenient for transport, since Goswell Road, at the western end of Moreland Street, led south to Aldersgate Street (the southern end of the old 'high road to Scotland', later the A1) and north to the Angel, and the main-line railway stations of King's Cross, St Pancras and Euston.

There was also room for stabling, for at this time the company still made its deliveries by horse-drawn van in the London area. The fleet included two vans with paired horses, and three vans with single horses. There had been no space at Ropemakers Street to house the horses and they were stabled in Spitalfields nearby. Although by this time internal combustion engines were accepted, and petrol-driven vans were common, the wine and brewing trades kept to the traditional methods of distribution. It is significant that the architect's impressions of the new building showed the roads populated with horse-drawn carts only, except for one man wheeling a handcart. It was accepted, though, that 'recent modern developments may some time demand space and accommodations for motor car requirements'. In the event, motor transport was not introduced until after the First World War.

The new building therefore required considerable ingenuity on the part of the architect – H. H. Tasker, an experienced servant of the licensed trade. He provided a five-storey building of brick faced with Portland stone, above a cavernous basement housing the great tuns. The central block was given over to offices, and on each side were warehouses, each with its own cart entrance leading to a loading bay at the back. The building was, however, modern in construction, since steel was used for girders and joists, and many of the columns between the floor were of solid steel. This was both because of the need to provide for the considerable weight of the vats (the largest were in the basement, but a number of 12,000-gallon vats were

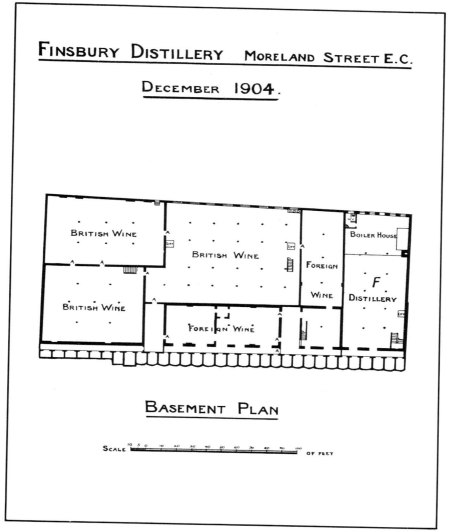

Plan of the Moreland Street Distillery, 1904.

positioned on the upper floors), but also because the firm wanted to allow for additional storeys to be built on top at a later date. The total floor space was over an acre.

The construction work was completed by the builder Gray Hill in eleven months, one month ahead of schedule, in spite of the considerable difficulties caused by the need to leave large gaps in the outer wall until the massive older vats had been transferred from Ropemakers Street.

The building in Moreland Street was efficiently planned. In the British wines warehouse, raw materials were hoisted to the top floor by electric lifts and cranes, and then the wine-making process continued in descending floors, until the finished wine arrived in the basement to mature in the largest of the vats, beside which was the bottling department. This was a manual operation, as it remained for many years. The practice of using corks was maintained because of a traditional belief that the reputation of ginger wine would suffer if it was not presented, like other wine, in a bottle with a cork that could be drawn. At the end of this process the filled bottles were hand-packed into wooden crates with rope handles (irreverently known as 'coffin-boxes'). The cases were then put into store: the stock of British wines alone was some 500,000 gallons.

In another section of the basement was the home and foreign spirits and wines department, with – says a contemporary account – 'hundreds of casks of port, whisky, brandy, rum and gin, and elsewhere thousands of cases of spirits, among the Scotch whiskies available being that of a favourite brand, Rothsay, of which the firm makes a feature'. In the storeroom on the top floor were 'boxes and bags of Greek currants, barrels of ginger from Jamaica, and hogsheads and bags of sugar from others of the West Indian islands.'

The gin distillery was, as the regulations required, in a section of the building with its own separate entrance and trading bank. The storage in the basement was 'vast'.

The argument for British wines was put vigorously in an article in *The Standard* (3 December 1907):

The idea, which is somewhat prevalent, that wine not made from grapes is of necessity not worth drinking is, to say the least, a very curious one. There is none of this prejudice in France, a wine country. Syrups are made there from cherries, strawberries, gooseberries, currants and other fruits in large quantities; they are diluted with water from drinking, and are much liked. If home-made wines can thus compete successfully with the *vin du pays* in France, it may well be asked whether they ought not to compare still more favourably in England with the cheap imported wine which has had to bear heavy charges for duty and freight. . . . It is better for both palate and pocket to drink a home-made wine when it can be depended on to be a genuine product of crushed fruit.

England was the natural home of these beverages, and, at the time when the Finsbury Distillery Company began its career they were to be had in great variety. Currants, raspberries, gooseberries, elderberries, sloes, bullaces, plums, mulberries and quinces were among the fruits. . . . Cowslip wine was highly thought of, and continued to be at least down to the middle of the last century. . . . Other kinds, some of which appear less inviting, were birch, turnip, dandelion, parsnip, barley, and rose wine. . . .

Besides exercising the skill which many years' study of their business has given them, the makers are proud of the fact that they use no chemical essences, and employ nothing but fruit and pure West Indian – not beet – sugar. On this head may be quoted an extract from the report on the ginger wine from a former medical officer to St Thomas's Hospital: 'I find it to be perfectly free from any ingredient likely to disagree with the most delicate constitution'. This was the quality of Stone's wines a quarter of a century ago, and the same quality the manufacturers guarantee is maintained at the present day.

A much larger quantity of ginger wine is produced

The old ginger mill in Moreland Street, believed to have been in use since the eighteenth century.

than any other kind. As few may know, it is made from currants, ginger being added to give both flavour and a digestive value. The currants, which come in a dried state from Greece, are steeped in water and subsequently crushed under hydraulic presses. These presses, which are worked by electricity, are immensely powerful; it is jokingly said of them that they could squeeze water out of a stone. The juice thus obtained contains all the goodness of the currants – a highly nutritive fruit eaten freely by the vigorous and healthy Greek peasants – and it is run down to the stores to mature. There it remains for a couple of years, when Jamaica ginger, which has been ground in a stone mill to fine powder, is added. After a while the ginger settles at the bottom of the vat, having thoroughly permeated the wine and rendered up its best qualities, and the wine is bright and ready for bottling. Made in this manner, ginger wine has an excellent flavour.

Ginger, moreover, is well known to possess the power of aiding digestion, and, taken as a liqueur after dinner, 'Stone's Original Green Ginger Wine' is not only a safe but an agreeable carminative. Diluted with plain or aerated water, it forms a refreshing draught, well suited in cases where a mild stimulant is needed. The experiment of trying ginger wine with soda water might well be made by many who have not discovered an entirely satisfactory lunch and dinner beverage. Notwithstanding its name, it is a fruit wine, and, for that matter, a grape wine. The *raisin de Corinthe* (currant) is, of course, a small grape.

Much the same process is followed in the preparation of the other sorts, comprising orange, raisin, black, red, and white currant, elder, raspberry, gooseberry, cowslip, and cherry. All the wines, except the ginger and the raisin, are made from fresh (not dried) fruit, and consequently they are manufactured only in the season when the fresh ripe fruit is to be had. With two exceptions – i.e. the oranges which are imported from Seville and the Valencia raisins – the fruit is all British grown.

Next to ginger wine, the most popular kind is the orange quinine wine, which supplies a valuable tonic in a most palatable form. . . . It cannot be too emphatically stated that these wines are in no sense 'imitations'; such liquors were made in this country long before foreign wines were generally drunk. In themselves they are wholesome, and those with whom sweet wines agree may drink them with the certainty of their being what they purport to be – a pure preparation of fruit juice.

In the upheaval of the move to Moreland Street, the Bishop directors had the assistance of Edward Stanley Ormerod, a director of Benskin's Watford Brewery (later taken over by Ind Coope) and a friend of William Henry Bishop. He became in effect managing director of the company, and held power of attorney for Mr Bishop in the latter's absence. His salary was paid jointly by the Bishop directors. There is a family indenture dated 31 December 1902 which sets down that James Bishop and William Henry Bishop would each be entitled to half the goodwill and net profits of the business, but that W. H. Bishop could not touch his father's capital. Perhaps as a gesture of family goodwill, William was allowed to delete from his contract the clause, dating from the 1860s, decreeing that he could be dismissed for unbecoming conduct (he was forty-seven at this time). It was further agreed between them that as long as Edward Stanley Ormerod was employed, his salary of £600 a year would be paid half by James Bishop and half by his son William.

It seems that the Bishops reposed considerable confidence in Ormerod, for James Bishop now only came into

The bottling department in 1906.

London occasionally from his estate at Newbury (which he leased from the Earl of Craven), and William Henry Bishop took the opportunity to travel abroad more often.

A traveller's book from this period shows that there was a further link with Benskin's Watford Brewery – the Finsbury Distillery supplied it with gin. Other customers at this time, many of which continued to prosper through the century, included Adnams & Co. of Southwold, Eldridge Pope & Co.'s brewery at Dorchester, Findlater Mackie & Co. of Brighton, and W. H. Cullen, 'Station Approach, Waterloo'. It is also recorded that in the years before the First World War, the Garrick Club was a particularly good customer for gin.

In 1909 old James Bishop's wife Isabella died at their

home, Hamstead Park. In the following year, James was eighty, and decided that it was time for him to retire. In 1911 he formally dissolved the partnership, though leaving in the business his capital and that controlled by the trusts set up under the wills of his father George Bishop, his brother George, and his elder son George Frederick Bishop (who died in 1898). There was thus no disturbance to the structure of the company when old James died two years later, in 1913.

William Henry Bishop remained as sole partner. But he was fifty-eight when his father died, and needed to establish the succession. He prepared to take his nephew Algernon Charles Bishop, second son of his brother George Frederick, into the business. Algernon had been educated at Wellington, and was, like his elder brother, Gerald, an officer in the Berkshire Yeomanry.

Maturing vats, 1908.

Before he could join the firm, war was declared in August 1914 and he went to France with an armoured car squadron.

The war changed a great deal (not least, the Defence of the Realm Act limited the hours of opening of licensed premises). In the Edwardian era, there had been a formality about the Finsbury office; it was still run in the fashion of the previous century, with clerks inscribing orders in great leather ledgers on tall sloping desks. The senior staff wore morning coats and striped trousers, and came to work in top hats or bowlers. The offices were heated by coal fires and the scuttles were filled by workmen who brought the coal up from the basement. The Bishop family lived in great style, and it was the custom that when deliveries of wines and spirits were made to the family house in Belgrave Square, the name had to be painted out on the wagon. It

The packing floor, 1908.

would never do for the neighbours to know that the family were 'in trade' – even if that paid the bills many times over.

In 1916 the company was financially reconstructed and incorporated as the Finsbury Distillery Company Limited, with a capital of £100,000 divided into £1 shares, of which 53,000 were held by William Henry Bishop, who became a director of the company. There was one other director, E. S. Ormerod; W. T. Ryde, the office manager, became Company Secretary, and R. D. Milner, Chief Cashier. Ryde was remembered as a hard man; Milner was tall, austere, but quietly professional.

Other innovations caused by war conditions included the introduction of women into the office and the bottling plant. It is said that they were warmly welcomed by the bottlers, but that as soon as men returned from the war their services were dispensed with as being 'too disruptive'.

The three separate departments were maintained in the new company: British Wine, Foreign Wine, and Distilling. Stone's Ginger Wine remained the mainstay of the British Wine department, although country wines including Elderberry and Cowslip were still produced in season. The Foreign Wine department bought in bulk in casks, and bottled wines, port and sherry mainly for sale to public houses and off-licences, then the main retail outlets. The Distilling department produced its own gin – 'Old Tom' and later 'Finsbury London Dry Gin'. There were also spirit cordials such as Cherry Brandy and Aniseed, and the list also contained imported Jamaica Rum and whiskies blended in-house to produce the Finsbury brand, Rothsay.

One of the office boys of those days, Morris Dickson, remembered in later years that he could always identify the type of trade of each of the firm's travellers who visited Moreland Street: there were those who called on off-licences, those who called on public houses, and the 'country travellers' who called not only on country off-licences but on the many local breweries then in existence,

One end of the despatch yard, 1908.

most of which had their own wine department, buying in wine and spirits from producers and marketers such as·the Finsbury Distillery.

Many men went from Moreland Street to the war, and the company treated them generously, making up their pay so that their families did not suffer hardship by their sacrifice.

Gradually W. H. Bishop, in his sixties, began to leave more and more of the business decisions to his managing director E. S. Ormerod. Though Bishop kept chambers in Albany, from which once a week he would visit the distillery, he spent more time at his country home, Farley Court in Berkshire.

Meanwhile Algernon Bishop had a war full of incident. Having seen active service with an armoured car squadron of the Berkshire Yeomanry, and served at the Gallipoli

Algernon Bishop as a fighter pilot during the First World War.

landings, he received a bad leg wound. As this effectively prevented his riding, and ended his career in the cavalry, he transferred to the Royal Flying Corps in which he was promoted to Lieutenant-Colonel (the RFC at that time was still effectively under army control and using army ranks: it became the Royal Air Force on 1 April 1918). He was for a time Commanding Officer of the new RAF stations at Manston and then Uxbridge; it was said that in the unrest and near-mutiny in the Services that followed the Armistice in November 1918, when it became clear that no sensible plans for demobilisation had been made, the one air station that remained calm was the one commanded by Lt.-Col. Bishop.

When therefore, on demobilisation in 1919, Algernon Bishop was able to return to the family company, he did so with a high reputation as a manager. He joined the Board, as he used often to recall, at a salary of £200 a year. From 17 March 1919 there was another ex-officer on the Board – Major Philip Forrester, a member of the distinguished port family of Offley Forrester. He was also a leading figure in that other great institution at Finsbury, the Honourable Artillery Company. Forrester had volunteered as a territorial, or spare-time peacetime soldier, with the HAC as early as 1909. On the outbreak of war in 1914 he was sent to Egypt as a Sergeant-Major. He served in the Middle East throughout the war, was commissioned, and later commanded a Field Battery. Several times mentioned in despatches, he later received the Military Cross for gallantry in action. On his return to London after the war, he maintained his service with the HAC and was promoted to Lieutenant-Colonel, commanding the 11th Brigade of the Royal Horse Artillery (Territorial Army), which included not only the two HAC Batteries but also the City of London Yeomanry Battery.

Algernon Bishop had double reason to celebrate his return to peacetime London. He had married (Violet, daughter of General John Leife of the Blue Marines), while on leave in 1916. In January 1919 his daughter Margaret was born. While remaining Governing Director, W. H. Bishop now effectively handed over the reins of the company to the new generation.

CHAPTER 6

Between the Wars

*A*lgernon Bishop and Philip Forrester formed a good partnership. They had both distinguished themselves in war, and carried the wartime camaraderie through to the peacetime development of the Finsbury Distillery. They broke down the traditional division between the office and the factory, not least by encouraging the formation of a football team. It was enthusiastically supported, even though it never won a match. Another innovation was the annual staff outing, generally by charabanc and usually to some popular seaside resort.

They tried to pick out and encourage members of the staff who could be groomed for higher management. One selected in this way was R. H. 'Peter' Piper, who joined the company at the age of seventeen, and was eventually appointed to the Board. He had some advantage, in that like Major Forrester he was a member of the Honourable Artillery Company. From time to time there was recruitment from outside, as when in 1923 O. T. Norris was brought in from Portal, Dingwall & Norris to strengthen the Board. But by the mid-twenties the firm had identified four department heads who were to give long service to the company – R. H. Piper, W. E. Lee (distillery manager), George Cowling (company secretary) and J. G. Pearce (British wine manager). Each of the last three were at Finsbury for more than fifty years.

The firm prospered. Sales were increased by the clever use of advertising. This form of promotion boomed in the 1920s, not least because of the success of popular news-

Seep eet
Drink eet
Drain eet

— being the famous "Sip it, Drink it, Drain it," advertisement for Stone's Ginger Wine as we overheard it recited by Monsieur De Canter on his introduction to Britain's National Comforter and Digestive.

Seep eet . . . .

Feel it tinkle on ze tongue, hein?
   Its warm sweetness
      And its sweet warmness
Clinging to ze palate
   Allur . . . . ah! delicieusement.

Drink eet . . . .

Is it not ze tres comfortable glow
   Inside you, yes,
It fill you wiz a sense of
   Ze bon life.

Drain eet . . . .

Je suis, tu es, il est . . . .
   Oh! la-la
It warm and cheer
   Ze very shell-fish—what you
say?—cockles—of your heart.

Monsieur De Canter

STONE'S
GINGER WINE

The ORIGINAL Green Ginger Wine—Famous since 1740.

papers such as the *Daily Mail.* For its advertising Finsbury employed one of the leading agents of the period – E. W. Barney, who was one of the founders of the Association of British Advertising Agents. It was Barney who invented the slogan to be associated with Stone's Ginger Wine for many years: 'Sip it, drink it, drain it'. His campaign applying this catch-phrase to different nationalities was successful in the twenties, though it sounds rather exaggerated to the modern ear.

The Frenchman, Monsieur De Canter, pronouncing 'Seep eet, Drink eet, Drain eet . . .' or the famous advertisement on the talkies –

> It shure gives a nifty nip
> To yer speak-piece
> Its comfortin' warmth
> Sorta curls around yer palate
> With a lovin' hug. . . .

– are scarcely credible today. Old Sam Barnacle the sailor is more believable as he claims that Stone's

> penetrates yer,
> Nor', Sou', East and West,
> An' warms the very cockles
> O' yer 'eart.

The leading figure of this advertising campaign, how-ever, to be associated with Stone's throughout the inter-war years, was the 'Merrie Monk'. This character appeared on the sides of buses, a prime advertising site – until objections from some churches at this 'irreverence' caused him to be withdrawn. The 'Merrie Monk' even produced a party book, but here again the copy-writer seems to have been stretched to the limit and perhaps beyond. The idea of having a 'theme for a party' is certainly a familiar one for

The 'Merrie Monk' in his green habit caught the popular imagination, but had to be withdrawn after criticism from the churches.

the period; but would any host succeed today with 'an Oriental Party'?

The invitations would be written in comic pidgin English; the decorations would consist of Chinese lanterns, and paper banners with supposedly Chinese writing on them. The guests would sit on cushions on the floor and the refreshments would be served in little bowls instead of on plates and in cups and glasses. Popular party games could easily be adapted to suit the theme. For instance, musical chairs played with cushions on the floor instead of chairs would cause no end of hilarity; and if there was anyone present who could twang a Chinese-sounding tune on a ukulele or banjo instead of having the usual piano, so much the better. The guests could be given cards bearing comic Chinese names like 'Hi Lo' and 'Ho Wat Fun', and these names could be worked into games and surprise items.

The simpler advertising copy, not surprisingly, is timeless because it relies on the truth about the product:

Have you ever tasted *real* Ginger Wine?
Do you know the genial warmth of it on a cold morning –its penetrating glow which warms and cheers the very cockles of your heart?
Stone's Original Ginger Wine is made today as they made it in 1740. It has been the favourite family beverage for nearly 200 years, radiating geniality and good cheer upon all occasions.

Or again:

You can't take the firelight's flickering glow to bed – but you can carry away with you the genial, friendly warmth of your last glass of Stone's Ginger Wine. Don't miss that goodnight glass! It's reminiscent of the crackling logs – it warms and cheers the very cockles of your heart – it's friendly, with an old-time friendliness!

The advertising was hugely successful, and in 1927 production of Stone's Ginger Wine achieved a record of 225,000 gallons.

William Henry Bishop died in 1928, and Algernon Bishop succeeded him as 'Governing Director', as the head of the firm was styled. W. H. Bishop was seventy-three and, while retaining an interest in the company, had for some years not been involved in its day-to-day activities. But it was a more serious loss to the working of the distillery when, in January 1929, Major Forrester died. His colleagues at the Finsbury Distillery shared the loss with his comrades of the Honourable Artillery Company. As the Earl of Denbigh, the Regimental Commanding Officer, said at Forrester's memorial service:

> There was scarcely an occasion on which he was absent; and whether it was duty, or some jovial gathering, his bright spirit and witty words gave a considerable amount of joy.... He took a leading part in the annual party given by the HAC to poor children of the neighbourhood at Christmas. There he was seen in his element, enjoying the fun as much as the youngsters.

To replace him, Wyndham Edward Hazelton was appointed to the board. He soon became the reliable 'anchor man' of the business, since Algernon Bishop spent a good deal of time away, either at his estate – Fairacres at Ingatestone in Essex – or indulging his sporting and sailing hobbies. He hunted, and was a good shot: in the foyer at Finsbury, almost as a mascot, is an impressive stuffed bustard which he bagged on the Spanish estate of the Williams

family (of Williams & Humbert). He also indulged himself in liquor. It became a familiar cliché in the office at Finsbury that after a Board luncheon the Governing Director would often tour the building and, if he was not in a good mood, would point at unfortunates who displeased him and say: 'You're sacked!' His temper could be gauged by the amount of silk handkerchief suspended from his breast pocket: if it was cascading out unrestrained, he was in a difficult mood. He was followed around on these occasions by Hazelton who would whisper to the victims: 'Ignore it . . . Colonel Bishop isn't himself'. One employee whom he did dismiss was his kinsman Harry Burns. Algernon Bishop rented a villa in the West Indies each winter and, once he was safely at sea, Harry would take himself abroad in other directions. One year Algernon came back early, discovered what had been going on, and abruptly terminated Harry's employment.

In the South of France, William Henry Bishop (Harry Burns's father) had entertained lavishly. As in the early 1920s he was still officially unmarried, Algernon Bishop's wife Violet acted on formal occasions as his hostess; this continued even after Algernon had fallen in love with an attractive Irishwoman, Margarida, the widow of Baron Oscar Ernst von Hausen (who later adopted the name of Howson). There seemed to be an inevitability about this, despite earnest efforts by the family to keep them apart. Eventually Colonel Bishop's wife divorced him and in 1926 he married Margarida. Relations between the various parties to this situation remained friendly, however, and their daughter Margaret (known as Peggy), dividing her holidays between her parents' establishments, soon became fond of her stepmother. The second Mrs Bishop had many stories to tell. She had been in Calcutta during an earthquake, and had ridden over the Andes on horseback. There was no doubt about Margarida's ability to charm men, and no doubt also of her intelligence and dynamism – which were later to be turned to the company's service. One of the great pleasures of Algernon Bishop's life in those years was his motor yacht *Margaret,* named after his daughter. (During the General Strike he sailed the yacht up the Thames, moored at Westminster and lived on board.) He did enjoy the luxuries of his life, and liked his little jokes. He would show his small daughter the brasswork on the dashboard of his Rolls-Royce and tell her that it was gold '– and all mine, all mine!' On one occasion, when driving to Essex to show her his new house at Ingatestone for the first time, he drew up outside a derelict hovel, braked, and said: 'Well, here we are. This is the house. . .'. As his daughter early became aware of his liking for luxury, this deception was not convincing even to a small child.

Meanwhile the Finsbury Distillery continued to prosper, through the General Strike of 1926 and the commercial slump of the early 1930s. Economies were required and the advertising budget severely cut back. Sales declined from the record levels of the previous decade and did not recover before or during the Second World War – it was to be twenty years before production levels surpassed the quantities manufactured in the twenties.

Throughout these difficult years, however, the traditional methods were maintained, symbolised by the great stone ring that was the key feature of the mill on which, tradition has it, ginger had been ground since 1740 to flavour the firm's main product. It was this historical tradition that most appealed to H. V. Morton, a leading journalist and essayist of the thirties, who told the readers of the *Daily Herald* in 1931 that he had wandered into a building of a firm which had been 'distilling something since 1740. . . . My curiosity was aroused.'

They took me to the great vats where men were making wine from a recipe as old as the hills. These were the sort of harmless but poetic wines which our Elizabethan ancestors made in half-timber country houses all over England.

Ginger wine is simply water, raisins, currants, sugar and ground ginger. It tastes much better before the ginger is added, but it is not, perhaps, so historically satisfactory.

No ancient drink would be right without spice. In Shakespeare's time sugar, spices, and even ambergris were added to sack, which was the popular name for Spanish and Canary wines.

The mill that grinds the ginger has been doing so since 1740 – five years before Bonnie Prince Charlie set the north on fire.

'We have found nothing better,' they said. You can mix those Finsbury potions with impunity. I drank a glass of raspberry wine, a glass of elderberry wine, a glass of ginger wine, and a glass of cowslip wine. This was the best. Cowslip wine is a pretty drink. If Titania drank anything it would be cowslip wine.

'It is drunk in only three counties,' I was told. 'Leicestershire, Nottinghamshire, and Bucks. It is not really a commercial success, unlike ginger wine, but we go on making it because we have always made it.'

The art of making this wine is to turn the subtle scent of the cowslip into a taste.

'We have to make our year's stock in May – cowslip time. Schoolchildren gather the flowers in the Midland counties. They come to us by the bushel. And they go back to these same counties as wine!'

The wine-makers of Finsbury agreed with me that it would be a good thing if more of these old lyrical wines were revived. Taste in food and drink varies, of course, from generation to generation. Ginger wine, I am told, is one of the few drinks that is more popular today than it was during the Georgian age.

I left Finsbury with the feeling that its wine-makers are keeping faith with the romantic past.

The romantic past, unfortunately, was not a sound basis for business practice and the Board – to which R. H. Piper was appointed in 1932 – kept constantly in mind the question of how long historically interesting but barely profitable wines could be produced. Ginger wine, though, showed no sign of losing its popularity.

In 1936 Morris Dickson, who had been with the company for twenty years, having started as an office boy at the age of fourteen, became British wines manager, and George Cowling succeeded R. D. Milner as company secretary.

The threat of war began to grip the country; and it was in these difficult days that Algernon Bishop died, in 1938, at the age of fifty-one (William Henry Bishop had died a decade earlier.) Shortly before Algernon's death, his wife Margarida was elected to the Board and this proved to be a most significant appointment. In the most challenging times she gave her heartfelt support to Wyndham Hazelton as he held the business together; between them they provided the motivation and drive for it to continue and to prosper. Though no longer young she used to come up from the country in her Rolls-Royce and take her turn fire-watching on the Finsbury roof during the London Blitz. (In later years, when economy was the rule, one of her juniors suggested that perhaps her car might be thought a little ostentatious, and that it might be tactful to come to London in something more modest. She was not amused: 'I have always used a Rolls-Royce and I shall continue to do so.')

Once war was declared in 1939, those members of the staff who had belonged to the Territorial Army were called to the services. Soon afterwards general mobilization took more men. The office staff were replaced by women for the duration of the war, but the warehousing and bottling staff were soon reduced to the minimum of older men, who formed a 'Dad's Army' to keep the business going.

The Finsbury distillery was fortunate in that it had traditionally maintained large stocks, and was therefore able to keep going by relying upon these. In particular, the large stocks of Rothsay whisky proved to be a particular advantage. But Finsbury was, of course, near the heart of London and, once the bombing started, the distillery was vulnerable. Considerable stocks were moved out of London and stored in the stables at Ingatestone, the Essex home of Lady Reckitt (as Mrs Margarida Bishop had now become, following her marriage to Sir Philip Reckitt).

By good fortune, the Moreland Street premises were little damaged during the war. Two incendiary bombs fell on the garage at the back, but these were soon dealt with by the staff on fire-watch at the time: the staff formed a rota and there were always staff on the premises, who watched with horror as great swathes of central London were destroyed around them.

A greater hazard to the business, as it turned out, was the difficulty of obtaining raw materials. Sugar and ginger came from the West Indies. Supplies of sugar were based on pre-war purchasing, and so made any expansion of production impossible. Sugar was brought in by the high-risk Atlantic convoys; everyone was conscious of the cost in lives. Early in the war, it was decided to concentrate on the production of ginger wine, and suspend the making of other fruit wines for the duration. The firm's buyers had to exercise such ingenuity as they could in obtaining supplies. From time to time, supplies of ginger syrup and glucose were found, which enabled production to continue, though not on the pre-war scale.

As the war drew to a close, one by one those who had been in the services were released to civilian life. In 1944 Peggy Maxwell, daughter of Algernon Bishop, joined the Board. So, on demobilisation, did Major Geoffrey Charles Bishop, son of W. H. Bishop's younger brother Charles

Willoughby Bishop. In the following year, Tom Pearce, a noted Essex cricketer, came into the business as a salesman.

Despite the war's ending, it was not easy to re-establish normal production. Supplies continued to be difficult to obtain, and essentials such as sugar remained rigorously rationed. The immediate post-war period proved to be no less challenging than the years of war.

You <u>must</u> be in on this

Stone's Ginger Wine has something of a reputation for smart advertising. But this season we feel we have gone even one better. The new advertisements we are putting out will tickle the public as much as Stone's Ginger Wine tickles the tongue.

We are very proud of them. So proud that we are putting them in all the newspapers in much bigger sizes than ever before. The reproductions in this booklet show the actual size they will appear . . . . . big dominating spaces with matter that cannot fail to be read, enjoyed and talked about.

Concentrate on lines that are well advertised. That is the way to success to-day. Concentrate on Stone's Ginger Wine. Show it well and let the great power of the Press work for you.

STONE'S GINGER WINE

FINSBURY, LONDON, E.C.1.

CHAPTER 7

A New Association

As the members of the staff who had been away at the war returned one by one, it seemed that the old order was returning also. In some parts of the business, little had changed with the passing of time. Indeed, there were some venerable staff who had started work at Ropemakers Street, and remembered the move to Moreland Street forty years before. Among them were George Cowling, the Company Secretary, and Harry Read, one of the clerks, who had started to work for the Bishop family in 1900.

Harry had not seen many changes, for bookkeeping was still in three-column ledgers, the entries inscribed by hand. The great leather-bound ledgers were wheeled up each morning on a trolley by three workmen from the strong-room in the cellar: the procedure took ten minutes. The ledgers gave details of each customer's account, divided into 'Town' and 'Country'. Other clerks would be seated at desks labelled 'Wines', 'British Wines', 'Distillery', and 'Transport Manager'. It was the job of the first clerks to arrive to sort the post and distribute them to the appropriate desks. Before any order was fulfilled, a check would be made in the ledger to make sure that the customer's account was in credit, or at least owing no money, before an invoice would be prepared in triplicate, one copy being sent down to the cellars for the consignment to be prepared.

It was some time before modern accountancy methods were introduced, first with a Burroughs machine, then with punched tape, and finally with the most modern computing system. Arthur Evans managed the ledger department on his return from war service, assisted by Miss Cluney (later Mrs Smith), who had held the fort during the war years.

Production methods were also traditional. For some years the company continued to use driven corks, partly because of the association with 'wine'; there were those who argued that ginger wine would somehow be devalued if traditional corks were not used. But gradually the message began to come to the firm from the retailers (in particular) that old ladies would buy a bottle of Stone's and ask the shopkeeper to draw the cork for them, because they could not manage this for themselves. The cork, therefore, was becoming a handicap in an important market, and so in due course was replaced with a stopper cork which needed no corkscrew to remove it.

Until the 1950s, Stone's Ginger Wine was still sent out packaged in the wooden crates or 'coffins' holding three dozen bottles, and taking two strong men to handle. After the war, many smaller firms that continued to do their own bottling were employing girls, who could not handle these heavy weights. The railways of those days did not always treat them with reasonable care, and there were many claims for breakages. When the trade did away with these mammoths, it was said that there was a bonfire on Hackney Marshes for a fortnight. The standard packaging thereafter became the case, holding a dozen bottles.

In 1952 Mrs Peggy Maxwell (who, as the daughter of Algernon Bishop, was the step-daughter of Lady Reckitt) was joined on the Board by her husband, Major George Maxwell, on his retirement from the Grenadier Guards. He had been in Australia as ADC to the Governor of Victoria (an association that was to prove of great value to the company), and his release from the army had been delayed by a block on retirements because of the Korean War. He began with the company as a salesman, covering Kent, Surrey and Sussex. It was a good introduction to the

The case-packing line in the early 1950s: note the open-topped wooden crates holding eighteen bottles.

business 'in the field'. After two years George Maxwell became sales director.

Gradually the business began to pick up after the difficult years immediately following the war: rationing continued until the early 1950s, and supplies of basic materials were seriously restricted. But with the beginning of a new reign (Queen Elizabeth had come to the throne in 1952, and her coronation in the following year was an occasion of great popular celebration), it seemed that better times were returning.

The new era was marked in 1956 by the retirement of three men each of whom could boast more than fifty years' service to the company – W. E. Lee, George Cowling and J. G. Pearce. Bill Lee had originally been a commission agent, and then a traveller for the company. He had been brought into the office during the First World War, had demonstrated his worth, and risen to be distillery manager. George Cowling was another considerable character: a meticulous company secretary, he was a hypochondriac who convinced his colleagues that he enjoyed very poor health (and existed on a diet of boiled fish and gin and tonic), but he survived into a long retirement to die at the age of ninety-six. 'Jerry' Pearce, British wine manager, was devoted to his job and convinced that development was being held back by the want of new machinery. Whenever a member of the family suggested some innovation, the usual response was that they had been talking to Jerry Pearce. Often they had, to his credit.

As British wine manager, Jerry Pearce would put on a bowler hat to tour the works, looking into the vats to judge whether a fermentation was bubbling; he would be able to see from its appearance whether it was ready or not. This traditional 'rule of thumb' – developed over many years' service to the company – was soon to be superseded by modern methods of measurement, but the skill of such men maintained standards by experience and judgement.

These long-serving workers were succeeded respectively by H. R. (Harry) Neave, Charles Reeve, and Morris Dickson. In 1957 the company took a further important step when the lease of the Moreland Street site, rented from the Northampton Estate for half a century, was bought from the Marquis of Northampton.

That year also the Finsbury Distillery moved into what was then a wholly new medium of advertising, and one that – at the time – was considered to be a highly speculative investment. It was television. Certainly television had 'come of age' by transmitting the coronation, three years earlier, and had then demonstrated – in black and white – that as a means of communication it was unsurpassed. With the establishment of independent television in the autumn of 1956, advertising time could be bought. It was decided to advertise Stone's Original Green Ginger Wine on television (the Maxwells bought their first television set to watch it). By modern standards the ads (still in black and white) would not be startling: one showed a girl circulating round a room with a tray of drinks, among which Stone's Ginger Wine was prominent; another (considered rather daring) showed a girl reclining on a sofa, inviting her boyfriend not to be cold, and have a Stone's.

The impact of the ads on sales of Stone's Ginger Wine that winter was immediate, direct and substantial, and production increased until in 1964 it reached 600,000 gallons, a record that was to stand for many years. (In the sixties, the company enjoyed something of a bonus from the huge success of the pop group the Rolling Stones: by the coincidence of the name, they were able to run an ad in which a boy, giving his girl a bottle of Stone's Ginger Wine, said 'What do you expect for fifteen bob – Mick Jagger?')

In 1958 Wyndham Hazelton died. He had been a director for nearly thirty years, and managing director for twenty. It is not excessive to claim that he was the company's solid and reliable guide for that entire period. He was unfortunate

Ted Dewing, distillery foreman in the mid-1960s, using a Sikes hydrometer to check the alcoholic strength.

in joining the Board just at the time when sales were turning down, during the great depression of the early 1930s; and he then had to negotiate the problems and difficulties of the Second World War. Indeed, it can be said that though he did not survive to see and enjoy the successes of the 1960s, it was his sound judgement and common sense that prepared the company to take advantage of the better climate that was to follow.

In the reorganisation that followed, George Maxwell became joint managing director with R. H. Piper. Charles Reeve, H. R. Neave and T. N. Pearce were appointed to the Board. Two years later, in 1960, Lady Reckitt retired from the Board, after long and devoted service, to become President of the company.

In May 1961 the Chairman of Showering Vine Products, Keith Showering, invited the Chairman of Finsbury Distillery, George Maxwell, to lunch. They discussed many things, and finally Keith Showering suggested that as his company had substantial cash resources, it would be in the best interest of both concerns if the two companies were to merge. George agreed to consider this proposal, but was not enthusiastic about it.

In the following two years there were similar discussions with Bulmers, Gaymers and Merrydown, but nothing of significance came from these discussions. The cider market was comparatively in the doldrums, and there were genuine reasons why no merger would be a sensible proposition. Bulmers was a family business, a private company; Merrydown, still in the development stage, was not then sufficiently large; and when the Chancellor of the Exchequer brought vintage cider into the tax net (almost by an oversight), he seriously damaged their business. Where Gaymers was concerned, its acquisition by Showerings pulled the rug from under Finsbury.

The fundamental problem facing the directors and shareholders of the Finsbury Distillery was that it was a private company with 85 per cent of the shares in the hands of three groups – Peggy Maxwell's trustees, and her cousins Geoffrey Bishop and Harry Bishop (formerly Burns), whose fathers were brothers. Believing that outside help was needed to find a satisfactory solution, George Maxwell approached Charles Villiers, an old friend and former brother officer, who was a partner in Schroeder Wagg (and who subsequently became chairman of British Steel). He was to prove of immense assistance, a wise man with a perspicacious outlook on contemporary financial trends.

In 1963 the giant Distillers' Company (DCL) bought Crabbie's, who had very substantial whisky interests, as well as ginger wine, and were as well known in Scotland and north of a line from Liverpool to the Humber as Stone's Original Ginger Wine was renowned in the Midlands and the south of England. With Crabbie's under the auspices of DCL and content to be so, it was mooted that the Finsbury Distillery might consider an approach to acquire the ginger wine business from DCL. Nothing eventually materialized from this.

In the spring of 1963 George and Peggy Maxwell travelled to Australia. The purpose of the trip was twofold: to renew acquaintance with friends made when George was ADC to the Governor of Victoria, and to determine whether there was any possibility of increasing sales from the minimal two hogsheads of Stone's then being sold each year.

Evidently the rival ginger wine was being imported to retail at 19s. a bottle, when gin was then only 22s. 6d. a bottle. In the light of this, it was obvious that Finsbury could never hope to succeed by importing, especially since the Australian wine boom was already beginning.

It was decided to approach various Australian wine merchants and vineyard owners to see if any of them could be persuaded to produce Stone's Original Ginger Wine in Australia. The most enthusiastic response came from Tom Angove, a producer of a leading Australian vermouth,

Photis Toumazis fills the spirit flagons for the London club trade in the early 1960s.

Marko, who consequently knew the secrets of infusions. He told George Maxwell that he was confident that he could deliver the goods, and on George's return from New Zealand six weeks later, telephoned with the satisfying news that he could comply with the requirements for the production of Stone's in Australia.

This was not least due to the fact that the growing of ginger had been introduced to Australia at the turn of the century, and that the Australians in Queensland had been able to develop a particularly good strain, free of fibre.

It was agreed that Angoves would produce Stone's Original Ginger Wine in Australia; this proved a considerable success. The opposition, still importing, was further handicapped because the Australian wine laws did not allow the wine to be coloured to their traditional green.

The five-year start enjoyed by Stone's was an inestimable advantage in the Australian market, and enabled Peggy Maxwell in 1978 to present to a leading Melbourne customer the millionth case produced in Australia. Although in the United Kingdom the greatest sales of Stone's have traditionally been in the winter, 'to counteract the cold', cold is relative, and Australians proved eager to consume this drink in weather they considered cold, but the British would consider only temperate, if not hot.

On his return home in 1963, George Maxwell was contacted by Charles Villiers who believed that he had found the perfect company with whom Finsbury should join forces. This company was Matthew Clark, who although never involved in production, had possessed a strong sales force in the drinks trade since the Napoleonic Wars. It had been founded by Matthew Clark, the son of one Charles Clark who, as Inspector of Imports at the Port of London, showed considerable gallantry and skill in capturing a gang of notorious pirates who, in around 1800, infested the Thames between Gravesend and London.

Having started trading in 1810, Clark's firm was soon well established and by 1837 had become an agent for De Kuyper, famous for their 'Hollands Gin' (nowadays known as Geneva), and for the respected Cognac house of Martell. The De Kuyper agency is held to this day on a handshake, and the Martell agency was only terminated in 1989 by the purchase of that firm by Seagrams. Records in the Finsbury ledgers trace the trading relationship between the two companies back as far as the mid-1800s.

Since 1946 Matthew Clark had been controlled by two brothers, Michael and Niel Gordon Clark, and their cousin Peter Gordon Clark, who by the time of the proposed merger had been joined on the Board by Guy and Francis, sons of Michael and Niel respectively. Michael Gordon Clark had a great faith in the future of British wine and had been one of the men who had persuaded the Prime Minister, Clement Attlee, not to nationalize the wine trade after the Second World War.

George Maxwell and Michael Gordon Clark both realised the mutual advantages of the merger, for in many respects their two companies were complementary and not con-flicting. From the outset it was appreciated that secrecy was imperative whilst negotiations were in progress. These negotiations took almost twelve months to complete, during which time Finsbury hived off a company, Maxwell Bishop, formed to develop gin sales to Ceylon – it did not prove successful. But by midsummer 1964 the negotiations were complete, and by early July the draft announcement was ready.

When the news of the merger was announced on 4 July 1964 it took the trade press by surprise, for this was an era before the massive takeover battles of the late 1970s and early 1980s. No Dutch auction had been desired by the parties concerned, and it says much for the acumen of the Matthew Clark and Finsbury directors that no rumours were leaked earlier in the year. This merger, which was to continue to be effective and profitable, was one of the earlier ones in the trade.

The Board of Directors in 1965. From left to right: T. N. Pearce (Sales Director), H. R. Neave (Export Director), C. Reeve (Secretary), G. L. Gordon Clark, Lady Reckitt (President), Major G. C. Maxwell (Chairman and Joint Managing Director), Mrs G. C. Maxwell (Deputy Chairman), Major G. C. Bishop (Deputy Chairman), R. H. Piper (Deputy Chairman and Joint Managing Director), C. J. Bishop (Assistant Sales Director), F. W. Gordon Clark.

CHAPTER 8

The Modern World

*F*ollowing the merger with Matthew Clark in June 1964, the business of the Finsbury Distillery continued its expansion along much the same lines as before. There were some changes of personnel: in 1964 another member of the family, Charles Julian Bishop, was appointed to the Board (he was to leave three years later, to pursue interests in Ireland), along with Guy and Francis Gordon Clark. Then in 1966 began the gradual retirement of the 'old stagers'. First, Morris Dickson retired as production manager: a precise man, he had worked at Finsbury since 1915. He was succeeded as production manager by J. E. D. K. (Doug) Smith: tragically he died suddenly in the following December, a particular shock to his colleagues since he had been an enthusiastic sportsman and body-builder.

As part of the rearrangement that necessarily followed, Lieut.-Comdr. Mike Chappell, a submariner through much of the war, who had joined the company as a salesman, was now promoted to British wine manager, and Henry Testro – whose acumen and flair in buying imported wines was now highly valued at Finsbury – became Foreign wine manager.

At this time the sales list contained a wide variety of wine and cordials, many of them still made at Finsbury. The list of Stone's British Wines comprised the 'Original Green Ginger Wine', and also Orange Wine, Rich Raisin Wine, Elderberry Wine, and Cowslip Wine. There were also Cherry, Blackcurrant, Apricot and Peach Wines (though these were bought in, and simply marketed). The range of other 'Stone's British Wines' comprised Ruby Wine, Sweet White Wine, and three British sherries – Golden, Pale and Cream.

The list also boasted a range of the leading Ports, including Vintage and White Port, Madeira and Marsala. Leading Spanish sherries were marketed, several under the 'Bishop' name, and also a good selection of Champagnes, Vintage and Non-Vintage, and Sparkling Wine. Other wines included fine Clarets, Bordeaux, and other French, German, Spanish and Algerian wines, in bottles and in jars. Ranges of Vermouths came from Australia, Cyprus and South Africa. The list of spirits was headed by 'Finsbury' London Dry Gin, which was distilled at Moreland Street; other proprietary brands were also marketed. The firm's own Scotch whisky brand was 'Rothsay'; once blended at Moreland Street (and a staple of the company's wartime survival, through the considerable stocks held at the beginning of the war), it was by this time bought in, having been pre-blended in Scotland. The list of brandies included most of the leading names.

Finally, the list of 'Alcoholic Cordials and Bitters' continued the tradition of the nineteenth century: still to be found there were cordials of Aniseed, Cloves, Cherry Brandy, Ginger Brandy, Lovage, Peppermint, Rum Shrub, Sloe Gin, Lemon Gin, Orange Gin, and Lime Juice Cordial. In the list of Bitters were Orange, Peach, Angostura and Campari.

There were some major changes in manufacture at this time. In 1963, the series of bottling vats into which the wine was put after fermentation were taken out and replaced by five large plywood tanks. In the following year, two immense oak vats were installed in the basement; holding 57,500 and 47,500 gallons respectively, they were believed to be the largest wooden vats in Europe, and were used for the maturing of the base wine.

In the sixties, George Maxwell devised another method

The two largest wooden vats at Finsbury, showing how every last inch of space is used.

of bringing the name of Stone's before the public. An enthusiastic supporter of the turf, he decided that the company should sponsor a race. In 1960 the idea of sponsorship had scarcely been broached, and so Stone's became a pioneer in the field. At first the choice of course was between Newbury and Sandown. But Newbury was then televised by the BBC, which was against sponsorship as it would 'display advertising on television'. Sandown was televised by ITV, and so that course was chosen. The agreement was that the race must be the principal race of the day, and that it must be at a winter meeting (since the sales of ginger wine are highest in cold weather: in 1963, for example, the weather was bitterly cold and sales of ginger wine escalated). The timing proved a double-edged weapon, since severe weather caused the cancellation of the Sandown meeting in three years of the sixties. With a prize of £2000, the Stone's Ginger Wine race was regarded at that time as one of the top steeplechases. The company was honoured that on each occasion the race was run (it ceased in 1979), the Stone's Ginger Wine Trophy was presented to the winning owner by Her Majesty Queen Elizabeth the Queen Mother.

The company's interest in racing dated back many years. Traditionally, the Finsbury Distillery closed down on Derby Day, so that the Directors and their business associates could use the delivery wagons to view the race.

Early in 1970 Lady Reckitt died. She had been President of the Company for ten years, and was remembered for her staunch and determined defence of its interests throughout the war. Shortly afterwards, Major Geoffrey C. Bishop died, the last bearer of the Bishop name on the Board (though the deputy chairman Mrs Peggy Maxwell, Lady Reckitt's step-daughter, was of course a Bishop by birth and a dedicated upholder of the Bishop tradition in the company).

By chance it happened that these departures coincided with major reorganizations within the Matthew Clark Group.

HM Queen Elizabeth the Queen Mother presents the trophy to Mr H. J. Joel, whose horse The Laird won the Stone's Ginger Wine Steeplechase at Sandown Park, 1967. George Maxwell, Chairman of Stone's, is on the right.

As a result of these changes, the marketing and selling elements of the home trade side of Stone's was transferred to Matthew Clark & Sons in 1971, and in the next year the marketing by the Finsbury Distillery of foreign wines and spirits was terminated. Indeed at this time Finsbury ceased distilling, since the last batch of gin was made in May 1970; the gin-making equipment was removed in the summer of 1972, and distilling ceased at Moreland Street, though the name of Finsbury London Dry Gin is upheld by its being made under licence; indeed, it is, at the time of writing, the second best-selling London Gin on the German market.

In part this reorganization was so that office-space could be created for Matthew Clark at 183–5 Central Street, at one end of the Moreland Street complex, to which Matthew Clark moved from their former offices in Walbrook.

The climate of the drink trade was now demanding high-volume sales. The old fruit wines – elderberry, cowslip – were no longer viable, and were discontinued (the increase in home wine-making in these years may have contributed to this change, since people who were eager to enjoy these traditional tastes were interested enough to attempt home wine-making). More significant, however, was the major transformation of the wine and spirit trade in these years.

During the 1960s and early 1970s the large brewery companies, formed in those years through amalgamations, began to expand their wine and spirit activities and take over the traditional wine merchants. At the same time, the major change in retailing patterns by the introduction of the main supermarket chains, and their move into the sale of wines and spirits, also threatened the smaller merchants. Most significant of all, there was the 'transport revolution', as it has been called:

> Even the smaller wholesaler used to buy much of his wine in bulk; a few hogsheads of claret, half a dozen 'pieces' of burgundy, some butts of sherry and a pipe or two of port. Bottled with simple equipment (or entirely by hand) and labelled with his own name, such wines gave the merchant a good profit.
>
> But those wooden casks could not be stuffed into a container or stacked on a pallet; they did not 'fit' into modern transport systems. So the hogshead was re-placed first by something called the 'safrap container' (which held a great deal more wine) and this in turn was superseded by the road tanker. The smaller shipper couldn't handle this volume of wine in one delivery,

and so he had to ship in bottle, glass and all. The cost of this became extremely competitive as handling systems improved and motorways were built, but again the system favours the larger importer. The economic unit is the 40-ft container which holds about 1,200 cases of wine.[1]

Following the reorganization of the group activities in 1970–2, several more of the 'old stagers' retired: T. N. Pearce, sales director, in 1971, and H. R. Neave and R. H. Piper in 1972. Tom Pearce was a considerable cricketer, a former captain of Essex and for some years organiser of the cricket festival held annually at Scarborough. He was also, in his younger days, a leading rugby referee of international standard, for which he was later awarded the OBE. A gregarious man, his extensive contacts in the sporting world were an asset in his work as sales director. Harry Neave was a bachelor, an enthusiast for the arts, and knowledgeable about ballet. He was a traditionalist, as were his colleagues.

Richard H. Piper, who retired in 1972, had been on the Board for forty years, in his later years as deputy chairman and joint managing director. Inevitably known, because of his surname, as 'Peter' or 'Pip', he was a big man in every sense, standing well over six feet. He was known throughout the company as 'a real gentleman'. Very well liked, he was dedicated to his job: so much so, that he would stay in the office until late at night, though a keen gardener. It was said that he would sometimes go home and mow the lawn in the dark, with the aid of a torch. His colleagues offered him, as a retirement present, a lawn mower with headlamps.

Following these retirements, Mike Chappell became production director (with Ray Thomas as production manager), and Norman Sims became export director. As production manager, Mike Chappell is now credited as having been responsible (encouraged by George Maxwell and 'Pip' Piper), for transforming the production style of the Finsbury Distillery. The traditional methods, which some described as 'a bit of this and a bit of that', the main decisions being taken on a basis (described above) of 'rule of thumb', were superseded by the more technical and research-based methods of modern production. Mike Chappell introduced wine chemists into the company, and taught himself enough about the chemistry of wine to be able to make sensible assessments of their recommendations. He could be brisk, with an unmistakable Naval directness, and he operated on something of a short fuse. On one occasion he was told that a firm delivering empty bottles had – contrary to instructions – sent a huge truck that could not manoeuvre into Moreland Street's old-fashioned delivery bays. He picked up the telephone and directed a strongly worded broadside at the supplier, ignoring the desperate semaphorings of his office colleagues. 'That should sort them out,' he said, putting the phone down – and had to be told that he had shot up the wrong supplier. . . . He promptly telephoned again to apologise, and then as quickly redirected his broadside elsewhere. Mike Chappell did not suffer fools gladly, and would issue the fiercest of reprimands: then he would put the incident behind him.

Another considerable character in the company at that time, also with a reputation for fierceness of temper, was the remarkable and admirable Henry Testro, Foreign wine manager. Henry had also served in the Navy, and joined the Finsbury Distillery in 1949, first as a ledger clerk (working beside Harry Read, who had joined Finsbury nearly half a century earlier). Appointed Foreign wine buyer, he soon began to ship 100 hogsheads of Beaujolais and fifty hogsheads of second growth Claret each year. His flair was obvious. Like many small men, and red-haired men, he had a notoriously fierce manner. One customer, who said that he did not much like the design of a bottle label and wanted it changed, was asked to speak to Henry. After a short conversation he was heard to say, much abashed, that he fully appreciated Mr Testro's opinion, and of

Mr Henry Testro – in his normal office attire – providing sustenance and warmth with some Stone's Ginger Wine!

course he now understood why the label was as it was, and why it would be most unwise to change it. Another representative of a distinguished house, touring the factory before lunch, rashly made some mildly critical comment and got a response from Henry that caused him to say to one of the directors: 'You have a *tiger* downstairs. . . .' But Henry Testro's fierce loyalty to Finsbury was matched by the skill, flair and wisdom of his wine buying, which the company had ample cause to value.

Henry Testro was also responsible for the 'Moreland Street murder'. It was an office joke that he and Charles Bishop were perpetually arguing, and that the sound and fury of their arguments caused their colleagues serious annoyance – none more so than the soon-to-be company secretary, Arthur Evans. One day the arguments seemed to be rising to an altogether higher pitch than usual. Arthur Evans emerged from his office to see Henry pull out a pistol and fire; and Charles Bishop sank moaning to the ground, clutching his chest, while a red stain oozed slowly across the carpet. . . . Arthur Evans was dialling the third '9' to summon the police, when the office began to laugh. There was, however, a problem of how to remove the red ink stain from the new office carpet. On the office reorganisation, Henry Testro became a highly valued marketing man for Matthew Clark, in which capacity he coaxed, cajoled and sometimes pushed his sales force into new efforts. He is not known to have shot any of them, even in the pursuit of greater sales.

As part of the company's rationalization, the decision was taken to concentrate on production of Stone's Ginger Wine, already a best-seller. This was partly due to the ready availability of raw materials (which had been in such short supply after the war, and indeed into the fifties, that the product had to be rationed on the home market). It was also due to a sudden upsurge of demand in the Caribbean in the early 1970s. The sales of British wines were increasing so

significantly at this time that the company considered
moving away from Finsbury, since the room for expansion
in Moreland Street was so limited. The group considered a
site at Plymouth, and a new factory was planned. But then
the Arab–Israeli war led to an oil crisis and a damaging
world recession. The Jamaican economy also turned down,
ending for a time the mini-boom in sales that had looked so
promising. Two years later, an agreement was made with
J. Wray and Nephew – on the lines of the Australian
agreement negotiated a decade earlier – to manufacture
locally, which led to a recovery of the sales of Stone's Ginger
Wine throughout the Caribbean.)

There is, of course, a local interest since ginger is an
indigenous product of the Caribbean, where it is believed
to have notable properties. According to the local advertising, Stone's Ginger Wine

> possesses the many qualities extracted from ginger,
> increases virility in men, stimulates appetite, increases
> sex drive, restores lost energy, increases blood flow,
> cures coughs, colds, is a general health tonic, is a
> refreshing, vitalising drink.

In 1975 George Maxwell retired as Group Chairman (a post
to which he had been appointed some two years earlier)
and Managing Director, on medical advice, while remaining
special consultant for the Australian market. In his time he
had seen great changes, and had brought the company into
greater efficiency to face the challenges of the last decades of
the century. Not the least of his contributions was to
introduce a logical chain of command. Mrs Peggy Maxwell
(who had been a director of the company since 1944) then
took over as non-executive Chairman, still intensely proud
of the Bishop tradition in the company. (The family link
was to be further sustained from 1976 with the arrival in the
business of Major and Mrs Maxwell's son Charles: he joined

the Board five years later.) Lieut.-Comdr. Mike Chappell was appointed Managing Director. In March one of the last of the notable figures from the past also retired – Charles Reeve, the company secretary, who could boast forty-five years' service to the firm. He was a precise, rather Victorian figure, and carried with him the aura of tall desks with quill pens, and leather-bound ledgers. Port was his particular drink, about which he was knowledgeable. As his successor, Arthur Evans was appointed to the Board.

There followed a period of considerable activity and development. Once again there was discussion about whether to move away from Finsbury to provide room for expansion. But it was realized that to operate the existing winery with its maturing wines, while building up stocks in an entirely new winery, would be very expensive. It was therefore decided to develop Moreland Street, with the conversion of the old Distillery area into a new office complex, and the conversion of the old Finsbury offices into a modern wine production layout, which incorporated a new mechanized bottling plant. This, with a capacity of 9000 bottles an hour (800 cases), gave a 50 per cent improvement on the old line. At the same time, the traditional cork stoppers were replaced by screw caps. There was some resentment among the traditionalists who believed that a bottle of 'wine' should invariably have a cork; but this view was not reflected in sales, which continued to increase. Later, this modernization led to similar improvements in packaging, when Ray Thomas (now production director) introduced shrink wrapping in 1982 (except for export packs, which continued to be despatched in cartons).

Within two years the necessary building work was completed, providing a new boardroom and a computer complex for the group. Soon afterwards as part of the modernization of the winery, a chilling plant was installed; the purpose of this was to remove potassium and calcium tartrates which, while not harmful to the product chemically, could, under certain climatic conditions, form an unsightly sediment in the bottle.

As part of the expansion of export sales of Stone's Ginger Wine, an agreement for local production was signed in 1978 with Andres Wines of Ontario, Canada. Because of the continuing pressure on space through the group's increased business, a fourth floor was built on to the Central Street offices in 1979. There was a further development in production in the following year, when a bulk storage tank was installed to hold the spirit used for fortification, hitherto obtained in the traditional drums.

In the following November, the managing director Mike Chappell was travelling in to London by train when he was suddenly taken ill; the illness tragically proved to be a brain tumour (to which the stress of his war service in submarines may have contributed), and he died some months later.

This blow sadly coincided with a general downturn in trade, and an inflation rate approaching 20 per cent. This was a depressing period which the company, in common with many others in the wine trade, was proud to survive. But with the upturn in the British economy from 1983, the modernizations in the previous few years – which had included the replacement of the twelve small vats used for gingering the wine, that had come from Ropemakers Street, with new ones of Douglas fir – began to bring their reward, and slowly but surely signs of growth began to appear. The investment of nearly £2 million in capital expenditure on buildings and plant in the decade to April 1985 began to show fruit. In export markets too, where there were increased sales to the United States and even to Japan, success began to appear. Though export markets could be volatile, in none was the success so marked as in Australia, where a 1963 sales estimate (perhaps optimistic) of 3000 cases of Stone's Ginger Wine per year had been turned, twenty-five years later, into a regular sale of around 100,000 cases per year.

The one millionth case of Stone's Ginger Wine to be produced in Australia, March 1980. From left to right: Doug Crittenden, Mrs G. C. Maxwell (Chairman of Finsbury), John Angove (Managing Director of Angove's).

With the upturn in the British economy, the supermarket outlets became even more successful. It was a tribute to the Finsbury Distillery that when the leading supermarkets began to develop their 'own label' brands in many products, it was to Finsbury that they turned when they sought the best ginger wine. The production of 'own label' ginger wines for the major supermarket chains was to prove one of the great successes of the company in the 1980s. It was founded on a sound reputation for quality.

In 1982 an article appeared in the leading medical journal *The Lancet* (20 March 1982) recording research results achieved by two American psychologists, Daniel B. Mowrey (of Brigham Young University) and Dennis E. Clayson (of Mount Union College), who published the results of exhaustive tests showing that the powdered rhizome of Zingiber Officinale (better known as ginger) helped to prevent the gastro-intestinal symptoms of motion sickness. Antony Charles Seeley, son of Queensland's Buderim Ginger UK agent, and then a student, worked this into an amusing article in which he commented that

> this will come as no surprise to those who already take ginger for colic, drink it for dyspepsia, chew it to relieve toothache, add it to boiling milk for gout and find it indispensable for the relief of colds – even as an aphrodisiac. The Chinese used it (and still do) to stimulate appetites, improve their bloodflow, cure coughs, colds, chilblains, burns – even an allergy to shellfish.

Soon afterwards Dr Oliver Gillie wrote an article in the *Sunday Times* (23 May 1982) quoting this research and that of Dr Charles Dorso of Cornell University Medical College, who had found that his blood was delayed in clotting – and traced this to a quantity of ginger and grapefruit marmalade that he had eaten the previous evening. Dr Gillie also quoted a fourteenth-century sex manual in which the use of ginger is powerfully commended as an aphrodisiac, a use that of course would not be claimed by the present manufacturers of Stone's Ginger Wine . . . or would it?

However, from 1984 the company began once again to invest substantially in advertising, specifically on television, where its new advertisement won an award; and this, supporting the general upturn of the British economy, enabled the Finsbury Distillery to satisfy increased demand, so that, by the end of the 1980s, the volume of production of Stone's Original Green Ginger Wine had once more topped 500,000 gallons annually in Great Britain, while worldwide production was nearing 750,000 gallons.

Among the advertising campaigns that attracted particular public attention was one in the spring of 1985, when a forty-eight-sheet poster appeared opposite the Law Courts in the Strand, in the heart of London, advertising Stone's Ginger Wine and making resounding claims for it, including those concerning its aphrodisiac properties. The campaign was launched (and ended) on 1 April, and at noon the poster was covered with an 'April Fool' sticker. A similar campaign was mounted a year later, when estate agents' boards appeared on a number of prime sites in London's West End, announcing that the sites had been purchased by Stone's, who needed the land for ginger plantations. City Hall, Westminster, received more than 100 puzzled telephone calls. In the next year, the campaign was repeated in various provincial cities.

Nor did Finsbury's inventiveness stand still in other areas, In 1988 Charles Maxwell, now managing director, commissioned a special Gallup Poll on winter, which demonstrated that

> for all its misery and discomfort, winter's still welcomed by a staggering 95 per cent of Brits who look forward to the joys of Christmas, winter walks, open fires, and getting out their winter wardrobe.
>
> Favourite winter warmers include hot milky drinks, soups and hot toddies. From the drinks cabinet come Brandy and Benedictine, mulled wine, and Whisky Macs made with 50–50 whisky and ginger wine (a particular favourite in Scotland where one in five adults choose it to fight the winter freeze). While, with the 21–34 age group, whisky and ginger wine are the two alcoholic drinks marked out as a special buy for winter.

In 1984 a special ginger wine, Exhibition 1912, was produced from an old recipe and quickly established itself as *the* de luxe ginger wine, sometimes called the VSOP of ginger wines. Auberon Waugh, a consistent imbiber of Stone's, was moved to remark:

> Stone's Exhibition is to Original Green Ginger Wine what a twenty year old Tawny is to the best Ruby Port. . . . My own rule is to drink Original wine by day, the Exhibition by night. A man can save a fortune on central heating that way!

Meanwhile export director Norman Sims managed to introduce to a number of the better bars in New York a drink made of ginger wine and orange juice, and marketed with the assistance of an 'orange stone' which 'strengthens creativity' and is 'extremely lucky'.

The members of the Bishop family in previous generations would no doubt have been surprised by some of these developments; but they could only be satisfied and pleased that the product they made over a span of 250 years continues to delight and warm a great variety of people in all the continents of the world. It is a natural product made with pure constituents, relatively low in alcohol and yet providing a strong-tasting drink. The technical definition of wine in some countries has militated against it, since ginger wine is a fortified 'made wine'. But its popularity over centuries is in its favour and, whatever the technical details that may complicate its entry into one or two markets, Stone's Original Green Ginger Wine has proved its worth as a historic popular reviver and survivor; and after all, as its present advertising states, 'It's what winter was invented for'.

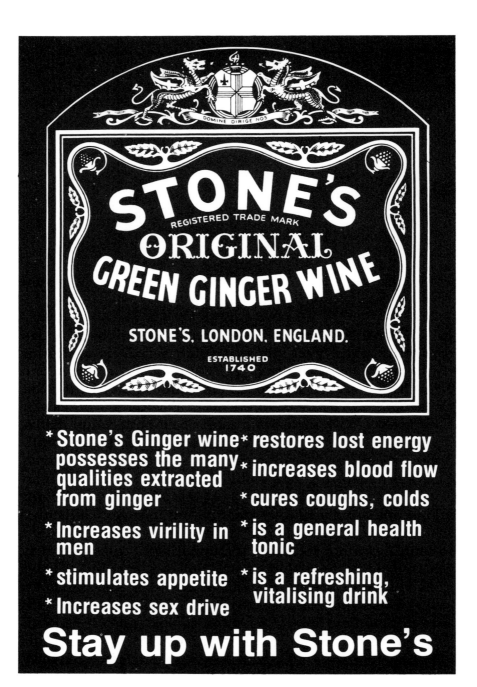

Postscript

*T*he growing demand for Stone's Ginger Wine presented increasing problems at Finsbury, where the age of the building, and some of the equipment (for some of the vats had been in use for over a century), made it difficult to plan for expansion. In February 1988 Matthew Clark and Sons (Holdings) announced that, from early in 1989, all production would be transferred from Moreland Street to the winery of J. & E. Mather & Sons in Leeds. Trial batches of Stone's had been made in Leeds for some considerable time and both the Finsbury Distillery and Mather were satisfied that no change to Stone's would occur as a result of the move.

To ensure an orderly changeover, Finsbury would continue to manufacture Ginger Wine throughout 1988, building up a stock of the product for transfer to Leeds. Thus Stone's would be made at one of the largest and most modern wineries in Europe, its output scrupulously monitored by computer, but still using the Bishops' original recipe.

J. E. Mather & Sons had been founded in Leeds by Joseph England Mather in 1903. He had been head brewer of a company manufacturing black beer, which was his first product. In 1912 Mather was prospering, but fell out with his partner and son-in-law. Mather sent him away, formed a limited company, and recruited his two sons Eli Bertrand and Rowland. From 1913 J. E. Mather & Sons widened its production to include cordials and fruit wines made from

The first bottle off the new production line at J. E. Mather & Sons' Leeds Winery. From left to right: Charles Maxwell (Managing Director, Finsbury Distillery), Tony Grayson (Managing Director, J. E. Mather & Sons), Peter Swain (Production Director), Ray Thomas (Finsbury Production Director).

locally gathered elderberries and blackberries, products similar to the range of country wines being made at Finsbury.

The sons both served in the First World War, but returned in 1918 to expand the business. When Joseph England Mather died in 1929 he left the business to his two sons, and Eli bought out his brother's shares. Eli's son Bertrand joined the Board in 1938, having taken his degree at Leeds University. Throughout the Second World War he worked in scientific research for the Ministry of Defence, but then in 1945 began to take an interest in the business, which he inherited when his father Eli died in 1949.

Output was then 20,000 gallons (90,000 litres) a year. Twenty years later, a new seven-acre site had been bought at Silver Royd Hill at Wortley, and the old wooden fermenting vessels and storage vats were replaced by large mild steel epoxy-lined fermenters capable of holding 25,000 gallons each and storage tanks similarly made with capacities of up to 90,000 gallons each. Bertrand Mather's plans were justified by increased sales: in 1966 output was 300,000 gallons (1.35 million litres). Bertrand Mather also contributed to the civic life of Leeds: first elected to the council in 1951, he was Deputy Lord Mayor and was elected an honorary Alderman. Over the years he made many good friends in the wine trade, George Maxwell among them.

In 1966 the business was sold to a consortium of Matthew Clark and Sons, Bass Charrington, and International Distillers and Vintners (Bertrand Mather remained as vice-chairman). Subsequently the company's expansion continued, and in 1988 the output reached an astonishing 20 million litres. Stone's Ginger Wine was thus joining a remarkable product list including Old England British Sherry, Chambard Light British Wines, and Moussec Light British Wines (transferred to Leeds with the takeover by Bass of the wine business of Colman's of Norwich). The Barchester Winery of J. E. Mather & Sons was also supplying British wines on an 'own label' basis to the leading supermarket groups – Tesco, Sainsbury, Asda and Gateway, together with other groups and chains.

This expanding production was monitored by a computer system developed at Leeds University, and partly financed by a grant from the Department of Trade and Industry. The successful introduction of the system was due in no small part to the fact that Mather's technical team was actively concerned in its software and measurement development. (By a happy coincidence, the language in which the programme is written happens to be Babbage, named after Charles Babbage 'the father of the computer', who was a friend and colleague of George Bishop in the Astronomical Society in the 1830s: so there is a link between the most modern system and the nineteenth-century Bishop family.)

There is a further important significance in this computer

system, since it led to a major change of practice on the part of HM Customs and Excise. Previously all winery products subject to duty were metered either by tank dips or calibrated vessels; these methods were not precisely accurate, but were regarded as more accurate than any meters then available. As part of the introduction of the computer system, Mathers commissioned a new twin turbine meter, accurate to within 0.15 per cent, and thus conforming to government requirements. The computer system is designed to take regular measurements of all containers, and the information is thus constantly updated. The new meters are standardized and regularly checked by an independent company. The regulations of HM Customs and Excise were changed to allow J. E. Mather & Sons to be assessed for duty on a basis of the computer readings, which the excise officers can check at will.

New buildings were planned at Leeds to help house the production of Stone's Ginger Wine, which would thus – while retaining its traditional recipe and character – be produced by one of the most up-to-date wineries in the world.

The ginger mill in its new location outside J. E. Mather & Sons, 1989.

Notes

Chapter One

1 Letters Patent of the Distillers' Company.
2 J. Samuelson, *The History of Drink*, p. 159.
3 Daniel Defoe, *A Tour Through England and Wales 1724–6*, Everyman's Library, Dent, London, 1928.
4 Defoe, op. cit.
5 Rudyard Kipling, 'A Smuggler's Song', *Selected Verse*, Penguin, Harmondsworth, 1977, p. 276.
6 M. Dorothy George, *London Life in the Eighteenth Century*, p. 43.
7 Parliamentary Reports (written by Samuel Johnson), quoted in M. Dorothy George, op. cit.
8 James Smith (1775–1839), 'The Upas Tree in Marybone Lane', quoted in *The History of Drink*.
9 M. Dorothy George, op. cit., pp. 322–3, note 41.
10 George Burrington, *An Answer to Dr William Brackenridge's Letter*, 1757, p. 37, quoted in M. Dorothy George, p. 323, note 47.
11 The original grant of arms is now in the possession of the Bishop family, having been returned after 150 years by a collateral branch.
12 Will of William Bishop of Grimston, PRO. It was proved on 18 May 1792, when his son Thomas had to swear that 'the testator did not die possessed of a personal estate to the amount of Two thousand pounds as he verily believed.'
13 Sir Arthur Bryant, *Years of Endurance, 1793–1802*, Collins, London, 1942.
14 George Rudé, *Hanoverian London 1714–1808*, Secker & Warburg, London, 1971.
15 B. R. Mitchell and Phyllis Deane, *Abstract of British Historical Statistics*, CUP, 1962.

Chapter Two

1 *London Gazette*, 25 January 1817.
2 *Dictionary of National Biography*, George Bishop.
3 *Report of the House of Commons Committee on Drunkenness*, 1834, p. 274.
4 André Simon, *Bottlescrew Days*.
5 J. L. E. Dreyer and H. H. Turner (eds.), *History of the Royal Astronomical Society*, vol. I, 1820–1920.

Chapter Three

1 Hurford Janes, *Stone's 1740–1965*.
2 A. E. Douglas-Smith, *City of London School*.
3 Douglas-Smith, op. cit.
4 Brian Harrison, *Drink and the Victorians*.
5 Harrison, op. cit.
6 Harrison, op. cit.

Chapter Eight

1 S. Loftus, *Anatomy of the Wine Trade*, p. 99.

The Bishop Family

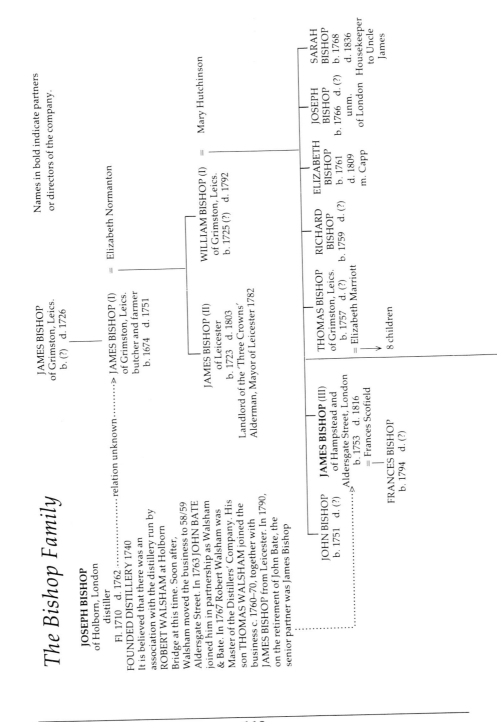

JOSEPH BISHOP
of Holborn, London
distiller
Fl. 1710   d. 1762 .... relation unknown ....>

FOUNDED DISTILLERY 1740
It is believed that there was an
association with the distillery run by
ROBERT WALSHAM at Holborn
Bridge at this time. Soon after,
Walsham moved the business to 58/59
Aldersgate Street. In 1763 JOHN BATE
joined him in partnership as Walsham
& Bate. In 1767 Robert Walsham was
Master of the Distillers' Company. His
son THOMAS WALSHAM joined the
business c. 1760–70, together with
JAMES BISHOP from Leicester. In 1790,
on the retirement of John Bate, the
senior partner was James Bishop

JAMES BISHOP
of Grimston, Leics.
b. (?)   d. 1726

Names in bold indicate partners
or directors of the company.

= Elizabeth Normanton

JAMES BISHOP (I)
of Grimston, Leics.
butcher and farmer
b. 1674   d. 1751

WILLIAM BISHOP (I)   =   Mary Hutchinson
of Grimston, Leics.
b. 1725 (?)   d. 1792

JAMES BISHOP (II)
of Leicester
b. 1723   d. 1803
Landlord of the 'Three Crowns'
Alderman, Mayor of Leicester 1782

THOMAS BISHOP
of Grimston, Leics.
b. 1757   d. (?)
= Elizabeth Marriott

8 children

RICHARD
BISHOP
b. 1759   d. (?)

ELIZABETH
BISHOP
b. 1761
d. 1809
m. Capp

JOSEPH
BISHOP
b. 1766   d. (?)
unm.
of London

SARAH
BISHOP
b. 1768
d. 1836
Housekeeper
to Uncle
James

JOHN BISHOP
b. 1751   d. (?)

JAMES BISHOP (III)
of Hampstead and
Aldersgate Street, London
b. 1753   d. 1816
= Frances Scofield

FRANCES BISHOP
b. 1794   d. (?)

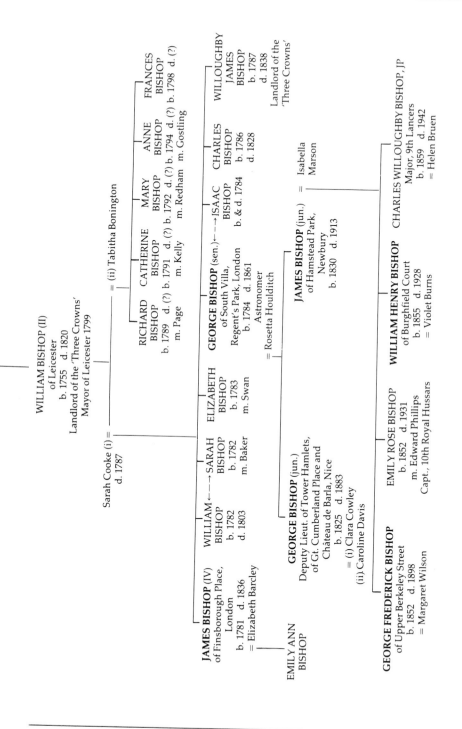

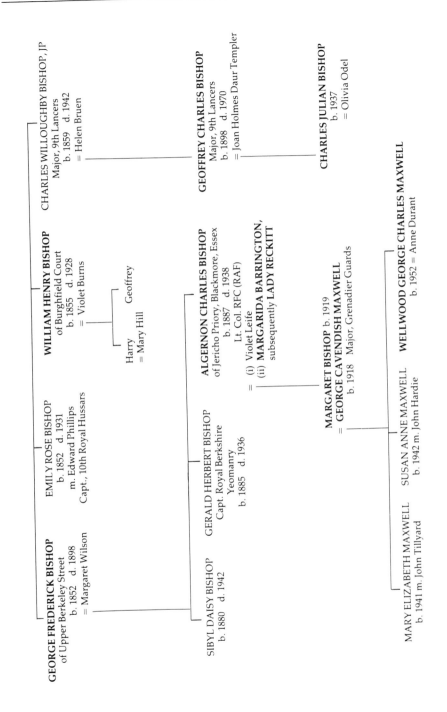

GEORGE FREDERICK BISHOP
of Upper Berkeley Street
b. 1852   d. 1898
= Margaret Wilson

EMILY ROSE BISHOP
b. 1852   d. 1931
m. Edward Phillips
Capt., 10th Royal Hussars

WILLIAM HENRY BISHOP
of Burghfield Court
b. 1855   d. 1928
= Violet Burns

CHARLES WILLOUGHBY BISHOP, JP
Major, 9th Lancers
b. 1859   d. 1942
= Helen Bruen

Harry   Geoffrey
= Mary Hill

SIBYL DAISY BISHOP
b. 1880   d. 1942

GERALD HERBERT BISHOP
Capt. Royal Berkshire
Yeomanry
b. 1885   d. 1936

ALGERNON CHARLES BISHOP
of Jericho Priory, Blackmore, Essex
b. 1887   d. 1938
Lt. Col. RFC (RAF)
= (i) Violet Leife
(ii) **MARGARIDA BARRINGTON,**
subsequently **LADY RECKITT**

GEOFFREY CHARLES BISHOP
Major, 9th Lancers
b. 1898   d. 1970
= Joan Holmes Daur Templer

CHARLES JULIAN BISHOP
b. 1937
= Olivia Odel

MARGARET BISHOP b. 1919
= **GEORGE CAVENDISH MAXWELL**
b. 1918   Major, Grenadier Guards

WELLWOOD GEORGE CHARLES MAXWELL
b. 1952 = Anne Durant

MARY ELIZABETH MAXWELL
b. 1941 m. John Tillyard

SUSAN ANNE MAXWELL
b. 1942 m. John Hardie

A Brief Bibliography

Chinnery, G. A. (ed.). *Records of the Borough of Leicester, 1689–1835 – Judicial and Allied Records,* Leicester University Press, 1974.

Douglas-Smith, A. E. *City of London School,* Oxford, 1937.

Dreyer, J. L. E. and H. H. Turner. *History of the Royal Astronomical Society,* vol. I, 1820–1920, London, 1923.

George, M. Dorothy, *London Life in the Eighteenth Century,* Kegan Paul, London, 1925.

Harrison, B. *Drink and the Victorians,* Faber, London, 1971.

Hutt, C. *The Death of the English Pub,* Hutchinson, London, 1973.

Janes, Hurford, *Stone's 1740–1965,* London (privately printed), 1965.

Loftus, S. *Anatomy of the Wine Trade,* Sidgwick & Jackson, London, 1985.

Mathias, P. *Retailing Revolution,* Longmans, London, 1967.

Nichols, J. *The History and Antiquities of the County of Leicester,* 4 vols., 1795–1815, republished Wakefield, 1971.

Report of the House of Commons Committee on Drunkenness, 1834.

Samuelson, J. *The History of Drink,* Trübner, London, 1878.

Simon, A. *Bottlescrew Days,* Duckworth, London, 1926.

Webb, S. and B. *The History of Liquor Licensing in England Principally from 1700 to 1830,* Longmans, London, 1903.

Williams, G. P. and **G. T. Brake.** *Drinking in Great Britain 1900–1979,* Edsall, London, 1980.

OTHER SOURCES

The main source of information for the later chapters of this book has been the documents and other information in the possession of the Bishop family and the Finsbury Distillery. Other useful sources have been the Leicestershire Record Office, the Guildhall Library (which holds the extensive library of the Institute of Masters of Wine, and also the Freedom Register and other records of the Distillers' Company), the Public Record Office and the London Library.

ACKNOWLEDGEMENTS

The initial research and work on this book by Michael Seth-Smith, before his sudden death, is most gratefully acknowledged.

We are grateful for permission from Sidgwick & Jackson Ltd. to reprint the quotation on pp. 100–101 from Simon Loftus *Anatomy of the Wine Trade*, 1985.

The prints on p. 5 and p. 9 are reproduced by courtesy of the Trustees of the British Museum; those on p. 7 and p. 24 with the permission of the Mary Evans Picture Library.

Index